AFRICAN EXPERIENCE

AFRICAN EXPERIENCE
A Guide To Modern Safaris

by
Craig T. Boddington

SAFARI PRESS INC.

The trademark Safari Press ® is registered with the U.S. Patent and Trademark Office and in other countries.

Boddington, C.

Second edition 2002

ISBN 1-57157-252-X

Library of Congress Catalog Card Number: 2001090819

10 9 8 7 6 5 4 3 2 1

Readers wishing to receive the Safari Press catalog, featuring many fine books on big-game hunting, wingshooting, and sporting firearms, should write to Safari Press Inc., P.O. Box 3095, Long Beach, CA 90803, USA. Tel: (714) 894-9080 or visit our Web site at www.safaripress.com.

CONTENTS

To my daughters, Brittany and Caroline.

My Africa is not the same as the Africa of those who have gone before.
Theirs will not be the same as mine . . . but in the diminishing wild lands
that remain I hope they savor a taste of what I have loved so much.

PREFACE

I am often asked to name my favorite hunt or, more pointedly, whether I prefer African hunting or North American hunting. The answers are neither obvious nor easy. We who are hunters cannot properly explain the feelings we have for our sport to those who do not share our passion. It is no small part of the essence of who we are, and while we do many things in the course of our lives we are always and foremost hunters. Throughout the world most hunters hunt the game found in their local areas, while some of us are blessed with the opportunity to savor large portions of the world's great game countries. Certainly I have been extremely fortunate, for I have managed to make a living writing about the things and places that we hunters love best. In that pursuit I have spent a great deal of time in the world's wild places—not only Africa and my own game country closer to home, but a smaller sampling of the other continents as well.

One of the things I have learned is that there really is no "better" or "best" place. They are all good. For hunters, any opportunity to exercise that portion of our being is wonderful. I love Africa, but I cannot rate days spent afield there as any better than the days of my youth spent following a good setter down those long Kansas hedgerows, nor the days I now spend hunting our California wild hogs or small-racked coastal bucks, nor better than days spent in the high country in pursuit of wild sheep. All days afield are wonderful, whether spent in a tree stand in my back forty or tracking buffalo in the Zambezi Valley. So I cannot tell you that Africa offers the greatest hunting experience, and I will certainly not suggest that a hunter is incomplete until he or she has savored an adventure there. I can tell you that Africa is fabulous, but beware: Africa is also a captivating and bewitching land, and most who taste it just once will long to return for the rest of their days.

The title for this book is apt, because unlike so many hunting trips Africa is truly an experience, offering a cornucopia of sights, sounds, tastes, and smells unequaled in our hunting world. My choice was certainly not the only possible title. "African Adventure" would have worked, because an African safari is truly one of the last great adventures in our shrinking world. I considered and discarded the emphasis on adventure because I have never been one to sensationalize— and Africa doesn't need hyperbole. It is an adventure just to be there, but it is also a fact that danger is usually remote and the hair-raising close calls we love to read about may not happen in an entire lifetime of hunting African game.

Depending on whether you view your glass as half-full or half-empty, another potential title for this book could be "African Obsession." My obsession with hunting in Africa started long before my first safari. My mother's brother, Art Popham, went on safari in what was then Tanganyika in 1956. Although I was very young, I clearly remember vowing that I would do the same someday. In the years that followed I read everything about Africa that I could get my hands on—John A. Hunter, Robert Ruark, Theodore Roosevelt, Frederick C. Selous, and all the rest. I was still quite young, not yet twenty-five, when I "finally" went on my first safari. That safari was to be my only safari . . . just to "get it out of my system once and for all." The experience was truly wonderful, but my plan to put dreams of Africa behind me didn't work very well, did it?

I have often joked that I would be money ahead had I started an addiction to controlled substances rather than embarking on that first safari twenty-five years ago. I have also stated, and it probably isn't a joke, that, as a hunting writer, I would be money ahead had I put Africa aside twenty-five years ago and concentrated on hunting white-tailed deer. The practical reality is that it is easier to convince the magazine editors I work for to purchase stories about game closer to home, for it is not nearly as simple to market a story on African hunting. Another practical reality is that, as a writer, I can't say with a straight face that I have ever made a profit from an African safari! Ah, but as a hunter, well, Africa has enriched me beyond my wildest dreams!

Many of you will be aware that this is not my first book on African hunting. It is also not the only book that has been written as a "guide to the modern safari." Regarding my own previous works and in a life controlled by never-ending deadlines, it is impossible to avoid some rehashing of events written about elsewhere. Over the years I have tried very hard to avoid such duplication, but I do make my living grinding out words. So some of the circumstances in this book have indeed been written about before. But I think you will find a difference herein. My previous African books have dealt primarily with very specific events, places, game animals, rifles, and cartridges. This book is quite different in that, except as examples apply, I have tried to avoid the specific; instead, I have attempted to wrap what I have learned about Africa in the context of twenty-five years. In that quarter-century I have been on more than forty hunts in a dozen countries, and there have been just three or four years in all that time when I only dreamed of Africa but did not journey there.

While I think my experience in Africa is extensive, I don't consider myself an expert, certainly not to the level of the many career professional hunters whom I admire immensely. Moreover, I do not consider my level of expertise the same to that of previous writers who have also penned "guides to safari." The difference is that most of those books were based on intensive experience in one or another region of the second-largest continent on Earth. I claim no such expertise . . . nor do I claim experience in all of Africa's current or potential hunting countries. I came along too late to experience Sudan, and I know little about the bulge of West Africa. But I have seen and experienced a great deal of Africa's diversity: I have hunted in most of the major hunting countries—and most of them several times—and I have hunted in most of the various types of habitat—and most of them several times. I followed no master plan; I was, simply, drawn back to Africa again and again. Based on the many safaris I have taken over the years, I believe this book will offer insight into what you can expect on a modern safari . . . and how it should be planned so that you can maximize the experience.

That said, there is a caution. One of the great problems with any book that generalizes about Africa and African hunting is that the printed word is final, unchanging, and enduring . . . but Africa herself changes on a daily basis. As I write these lines, the ink is not dry on the final chapters, but the face of African hunting has changed yet again. Zambia is now closed to hunting, Botswana has closed lion hunting, and Zimbabwe's internal difficulties are much in the news. The temptation these past few weeks has been to go back and revise things here and there . . . but there is little utility in that, because Africa would change yet again before those lines saw the light of day. Change is constant in Africa, so I would urge you to regard anything written just yesterday as already dated and requiring current verification.

For this book, I will stand on my African experience of these past twenty-five years. Whether you're considering your first African safari, or planning your umpteenth, I hope that the following chapters will be useful for you. And I wish you an African experience as rewarding as mine has been.

Craig Boddington
Paso Robles, California
June 2001

PART I

THE SAFARI INDUSTRY

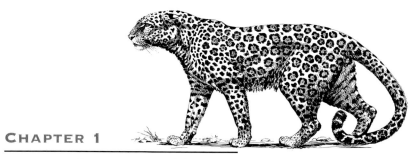

CHAPTER 1

SUNSET IN EAST AFRICA

The African safari is deeply rooted in tradition. Like everything else in this century, the business of conducting safaris has changed, but it's important to understand where we came from and where we are going.

The year 1999 was a watershed year. It marked the end of the millennium, but it also marked the hundredth anniversary of Ernest Hemingway's birth. This is important to guys like me, who have English degrees and make a living peddling words in the English language. But it is also important for all of us who love Africa, because in honor of Hemingway's hundredth birthday his second African book, *True at First Light,* was published. He wrote this book after his final safari in 1953. The handwritten manuscript (along with thousands of other manuscript pages) gathered dust for more than forty years, until the author's son Patrick Hemingway dusted it off and edited it for publication. It may be the very last word on the classic East African safari as it once was.

The African safari developed in a time when the human population was small and the game country limitless. From pre-Roman times, Western man was aware that lions and elephants roamed the vastness of the Dark Continent, but it was Cornwallis Harris who first stirred European interest in African hunting in the 1830s. In those days there were no safaris; there were genuine explorations with some great hunting on the side. In the fashion of the day, the explorers would write their memoirs and tantalize the imagination. This was the practice through the remainder of the nineteenth century. By its close, Africa had been largely explored, and the writings of Harris, Gordon-Cumming, Baker, Speke, Selous, and many others had made European and American hunters aware of the wonders of Africa. But the first modern safari was yet to come.

The honor of making the first safari goes to Theodore Roosevelt. He was not the first wealthy man to journey to Africa for hunting sport. But in 1909 he was one of the most famous and popular men in the world, and he was a prolific writer with the outlets to tell the world about his experience. Had he stood for reelection in 1908, he probably would have won. Instead, he chose to take his son Kermit on an extended safari in East Africa. The safari lasted some nine months and

On the edge of Tsavo Park in 1977, sights like this were common. Take a look at some of the lovely tusks showing on these elephants! Within a year after the closure of Kenya, most of the elephants were gone—and gone forever were the days when you would find them in open country.

took him from Mombasa all the way through Kenya, into Sudan, and finally down the Nile.

In Roosevelt's day the land was limitless and restrictions few. Colonel Paterson had taken care of the Tsavo man-eaters a few years earlier, and the party was able to travel by railroad to Nairobi. From there the journey upcountry required hundreds of porters, and they measured progress in just a few miles per day. There were no professional hunters as we know them, but there were settlers and farmers who hunted. None could leave their farms for the duration of the Roosevelt safari, but Roosevelt, through his friend Frederick Courteney Selous, was aided by some of the finest hunters in East Africa. Among them were the great lion hunter Leslie Tarlton and young Philip Percival ("Pop"), who later outfitted Ernest Hemingway in 1934 and in 1953.

In 1909 Kenya Colony was not Roosevelt's only choice for a safari, but it was probably his best. He made his choice on the advice of Selous. As a young man Selous hunted elephant in southern Africa in the 1870s, and in the 1890s he led Cecil John Rhodes's Pioneer Column into what would become Rhodesia. At the turn of the century Selous explored East Africa for the British, and it is almost certain that he recommended to Roosevelt the best game country he knew. By 1908 the game of South Africa had been badly depleted by the ravages of her pioneer era and two Boer Wars. Both Northern and Southern Rhodesia had fine game, but the country was heavy thornbush and was difficult to hunt. East Africa, with its high, cool plains, was relatively easy. Its forests and thornbush were broken by broad savannas. And it held an incredible variety of game.

The Roosevelt safari was remarkably lengthy, but it is important to remember that they covered most of the ground on foot. From a hunting standpoint, the safari was a spectacular success. They took elephant, lion, buffalo, rhino,

Short-grass savannas are relatively uncommon everywhere except in parts of East Africa.

and leopard, and in addition virtually the full range of common plains game, as well as a spectacular selection of rarities. Kermit shot a bongo in Kenya's high forests—a cow, but in those days the distinction was not as it is today. After incredible effort, Theodore took a Lord Derby giant eland in southwestern Sudan. They did it all, and Roosevelt's book *African Game Trails* told it all.

With a wealth of wildlife, relatively open country, and stability under British rule, Kenya became the birthplace of the modern safari. Trucks soon replaced the hundreds of porters, and safaris could wander far and wide throughout Kenya in much shorter periods. After World War I Tanganyika passed from German to British rule, and it became common for safaris to wander back and forth between the two colonies, expanding the variety of country and game even more.

Mind you, safari country was big, but the safari industry was still small. In dollars, costs were laughable compared to today, but those dollars do not compare with today's. Before World War II an African safari required a long sea voyage to Mombasa, a trip by rail to Nairobi, and then a slow journey over rough roads (or no roads) into game country that even then was receding. Safari was the province of the very wealthy, and in those days before the anti-hunters held sway, anyone who was really *someone* "went out to Africa."

Ah, but these were the safaris that gave us our dreams of Africa. Ernest Hemingway's safari yielding *The Green Hills of Africa* was typical. It took place when most of the world was in the throes of the Great Depression. Under the guidance of the great Philip Percival, the party left Nairobi and cut a wide swath down through Tanganyika, hunting here and camping there, going to special spots that only "Pop" knew about. They ended up far to the south and west, where the "*Green Hills* safari" concluded with fine sable antelope and greater kudu.

World War II gave the game a rest, but in the late 1940s safari hunting started again at an unprecedented level, with air service delivering clients straight to Nairobi. For the first time Americans, with new affluence and even newer world awareness, were the primary market. Even so, it was some years before there were noticeable changes in the classic East African safari. Nairobi remained the jumping-off point, with some safaris remaining in Kenya, others journeying south into Tanganyika, some hunting both countries, and a few traveling up-country into Uganda.

Fortunately for us all, the tradition of going on safari and writing about it continued. Hemingway's *Green Hills of Africa* is a "must-read" for anyone headed for Africa, and now that his 1953 safari has finally seen the light of day, so is *True at First Light*. But it was 1952, the year of my birth, that produced what is, to me, the best of all safari books. Robert

Geoff Broom and the author look out across the Great Rift Valley at Mto-wa-Mbu, one of the areas Ruark hunted on his Horn of the Hunter *safari. The advantages of East Africa have always included scenic beauty and availability of relatively open country.*

Ruark's *Horn of the Hunter* is, in the tradition of Africana, simply a chronicle of Ruark's first safari. But if you don't have a desire to go to Africa, Ruark's wonderfully descriptive prose will make you want to go. If you have the desire, *Horn* will make you desperate for the day to arrive. And if you've already been, it will bring it all back one more time.

Ruark's safari was fairly typical for the 1950s. In the company of young Harry Selby (who had apprenticed with Philip Percival), Bob and Virginia Ruark outfitted in Nairobi, then drove south across Kenya and into Tanganyika. From there they wandered down through Masailand, stopping to hunt for a few days or weeks at some of Selby's secret places. The bag was spectacular, though not unusual for the day. Ruark got his two lion, a couple of huge buffalo, a big leopard, a fine black rhino, and a good assortment of plains game. Although they hunted hard for a greater kudu, he did not get one—not unusual for East Africa, where the "gray ghosts" have always been scarce. They did not hunt elephant until Ruark's second safari a year later, up into Kenya's northern frontier district, where he popped a 110-pounder right off the bat.

Although I was very young, I clearly remember when my uncle, Art Popham, went to Tanganyika in 1956. His professional hunter was Stan Lawrence-Brown, and also in the party was young Dave Ommaney, who would later become "Winchester's man in Africa." That safari, too, was typical for the day. Art took his two lion, a buffalo, an 80-pound tusker, and a wide assortment of plains game—business as usual back then.

The accounts of great safaris of yesteryear are worth reading, but there is the danger of disappointment in reading too much into them. It was the great East African safaris that gave us the great literature of Africa and created the tradition of safari hunting, but things have changed a great deal.

In the 1950s much of East Africa was still a tree heavy with fruit, ready to be picked, and a safari could range from the lowest branches to the highest. A hunting license was required, but the cost was minimal and the bag limit, by today's standards, shocking. Armed with a hunting license for Kenya or Tanganyika (or both), a safari with a hunting car and a sturdy lorry could wander hundreds of miles at will. As Ruark did, you could hunt for a few days in an area good for lion, then pack up and move a few dozen or a couple of hundred miles and hunt an area better for leopard or kudu. Roads were bad, and it took much time to make these moves, but safaris were longer and less hurried then. Also, the game was plentiful and relatively undisturbed. Once in the right area for the game you were hunting, it took less time to actually find it.

Exclusive concessions were unheard of and unnecessary. The safari business was growing, but it was still unusual to encounter another safari. If you did, you would just travel a bit farther to camp. There was plenty for all and no competition. Permanent camps were also unheard of. The elaborate tent camp of the classic East African safari could be packed up and loaded into a truck in a few hours. Typically the truck would be sent ahead to set up a new camp, while the clients and the professional hunter would take their time, hunting their way to the new area, perhaps fly camping for a night.

The tradition of the mobile camp lasted until Kenya closed, but by the latter years things had changed significantly. In time, with growing human populations, shrinking game country, and increasing hunting pressure, the freewheeling days came to an end. Governments divided available game country into blocks, and hunters reserved the blocks in advance through the game department. This was the situation when I first hunted Kenya just before the closure in 1977, a pivotal event. By then Kenya was heavily settled, and I saw no game on the

Mobile camps, standard in the old days of East African safari, are rare today. In 2001 Alain Lefol used a mobile camp in Chad to cover more ground in his vast area, but most safaris today are from fixed camps in established concessions.

long drives to and between areas. We spent a wonderful week up on Mount Kenya, then packed up camp and sent the lorry ahead to the country south of Voi, near the Tanzanian border. It was a wonderful safari, but even then it was not the same Africa Ruark had written about.

Kenya's Mau Mau panic of the 1950s was a sad and messy chapter, but in its aftermath independence came peacefully. The transition was relatively smooth, and, at least for the safari industry, the changes it brought were not sweeping. However, the government opened to settlement much land that had formerly been maintained as game reserves, and many great hunting blocks ceased to exist. In the early 1970s Tanzania closed hunting, and Uganda's small safari industry ground to a halt under Idi Amin's paranoid rule, though the country never

East Africa has always been famous for wonderful buffalo, and they still exist. The author took this superb bull at Mto-wa-Mbu, Masailand, with Geoff Broom in 1993.

officially closed. This left Kenya alone as the last bastion of the traditional safari, but even Kenya was not the same. In 1973 she closed elephant hunting. This was certainly the beginning of the end, if not the end. Safari hunting continued for four more years, but hunting blocks were more limited and good blocks ever more scarce. At the end, bag limits had been greatly reduced, and trophy fees had increased to prices that would seem familiar today. But Kenya was still Kenya, and on the strength of her tradition and reputation it was there that I chose to make my first safari.

I'm glad that I did. It was a wonderful experience, still a traditional safari. Had I gone elsewhere, I would never have hunted buffalo under the tall trees on Mount Kenya, nor would I have seen a mobile tent camp. I know now that the

Lesser kudu was considered common game back in the days when East Africa was wide open. Today it is a rarity, available in just a handful of hunting concessions.

game was scarce, but overall I did pretty well. And of course one's first safari is always a shining memory, the safari against which all that follow will be judged. Mine was good. In real terms it was not as good as some that would follow, but it changed my life forever.

When Kenya closed all hunting in 1977, without a doubt this ended the era of the classic East African mobile safari. The hunting world was shocked beyond belief, and many good operators never recovered from the sudden and unanticipated loss of their livelihood. The late 1970s were grim days for the safari industry, and the closing of Kenya seemed almost a final nail in the coffin. Tanzania was still closed and Uganda was a nightmare. And East Africa wasn't the only problem area.

During the 1960s the Portuguese colonies of Angola and especially Mozambique had become popular safari destinations. After publication of his novel *Uhuru*, Robert Ruark was no longer welcome in former British East Africa. Prior to his death in 1965 he made his last safaris into Mozambique, where he finally found the kudu that had eluded him for so long in East Africa. But the safari industry was short-lived in both Mozambique and Angola. Hastened by a rapidly spreading bush war, the Portuguese pulled out in the early 1970s. Sport hunting quickly became untenable, and the wildlife of both countries would be ravaged by long and bitter civil war.

In the French sphere of influence, hunting continued in Cameroon and Central African Republic, but civil war in Chad ended the great hunting to be found there. Sudan remained open for several years, but now the specter of elephant poaching on a near-continental scale was added to the widespread political strife. It has been widely documented that the government of Kenya closed hunting largely to give poaching teams, sponsored by government officials, free rein in the back country. Within months of the closure, Kenya's great elephant herds had been greatly reduced, and virtually all of her black rhinos were eradicated. The same fate befell the great elephant herds of southern Sudan and Central Africa and, within a few years, those of Tanzania and Zambia as well.

The late 1970s were clearly a low point in African hunting, and all appeared gloom and doom. However, one must appreciate that in 1977 Kenya was not the only hunting country in Africa and almost certainly no longer the best hunting grounds. Although Chad was lost and the elephant herds would shrink dramatically, hunting remained good and very "business as usual" in C.A.R. (then C.A.E.) and Cameroon. Sudan, too, remained good until her own civil war forced closure in the 1980s. Although these remote, difficult areas never rivaled East Africa in terms of market share of the safari industry, they must not be overlooked as great and traditional

A very good fringe-eared oryx, taken in Kenya just weeks before the 1977 closure. Hunters in those days had to hunt hard to find their game, but the quality was still very good.

Greater kudu has never been common in East Africa, and was the Holy Grail of many safaris. The author got lucky in 1988, taking this fine bull in Masailand with Michel Mantheakis.

hunting countries. But long before Kenya closed, the industry was already starting to look south.

In the 1960s, concerned over the change in government and ever-shrinking game country, a few enterprising East African professional hunters started to explore new hunting grounds. John Kingsley-Heath and Harry Selby were among the Kenya hunters who set up shop in Botswana, formerly Bechuanaland. Others, including Dave Ommaney and Mike Rowbotham, wound up in Zambia, formerly Northern Rhodesia. In both countries they found superb general-bag hunting that perhaps didn't rival the very best days in East Africa but was certainly better than what remained in 1977.

Despite the long bush war, sport hunting was also starting up in Rhodesia. Pioneer outfitters like Ian Henderson, Brian Marsh, Peter Johnstone, and Geoff Broom conducted safaris literally throughout the war years, setting the stage for what would grow to a giant safari industry when the war finally ended in 1979. Farther south, South Africa's game was slowly rebuilding, aided by a new concept called game ranching. Namibia, then South-West Africa, continued to offer excellent plains-game hunting and was the primary destination for German-speaking hunters.

In 1981 Tanzania reopened hunting, initially through the government's Tanzania Wildlife Corporation (Tawico), only later allowing concessions to other outfitters. Tanzania would quickly regain its rightful place as a primary safari country, offering one of the largest varieties of game in Africa, some of the most scenic country, and without question some of the finest hunting. But it was not and never again would be the same. Gone forever were the days of the freewheeling safaris that could travel the length and breadth of East Africa. In their place came the era of exclusive concessions and permanent camps. The reopening of Tanzania brought back hunting in East Africa, and it remains wonderful to this day; but I doubt that the center of the safari industry will ever again shift to East Africa. In that four-year period between the closure of Kenya and the reopening of Tanzania, the safari industry shifted south, where I believe it will remain so long as there is hunting in Africa.

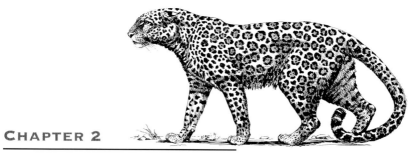

CHAPTER 2

SAFARIS MOVE SOUTH

East Africa was gone . . . and the southern countries were ready to step in.

It is not as though someone switched the light off in Kenya and turned on another lamp in southern Africa. By the mid-1970s Tanzania was closed, Uganda was finished, and Mozambique was in chaos. Kenya's elephant hunting was already closed, and the really good hunting blocks were few and far between. There was already a viable and active safari industry in both Zambia and Botswana, and old East African hunters were well represented among the handful of outfitters in both countries. As a genuine industry, safari hunting got started after Bechuanaland became Botswana in 1966 and Northern Rhodesia became Zambia in 1964, but hunting was hardly new to either country. Both countries had hosted a small number of visiting hunters for many years, adventurers who largely self-outfitted into the Kalahari for gemsbok, into Okavango for sitatunga and red lechwe, and into Zambia for black and Kafue lechwe, puku, and her other prizes.

It was a revelation to the world when, in 1961, a United Nations team described Bechuanaland as Africa's greatest remaining wildlife reservoir. I doubt this was startling news to veteran professional hunters across the continent. They knew what was there, but it was a different world back then. The safari industry was small, and so was its potential clientele. African safaris were lengthy and expensive affairs, and there was no Safari Club to beat the drum. There was good hunting in southern Africa, and undoubtedly a safari industry would have sprung up in due time. But in my view the decline of East Africa was the catalyst, drawing south not only experienced professional hunters but, more important, hunting clients.

Zambia and Botswana were not the only opportunities. The long bush war was ongoing in Rhodesia, and while it discouraged many potential clients, it didn't stop them all, nor did it stop Rhodesian hunters from grabbing their own piece of the action. In fact, Rhodesia was the scene for some of the first mass-marketing of short, packaged safaris. Surely you remember the ads proclaiming "Africa for $1,995"? In those days you could have the airplane ticket, a week's hunting, and a sable, a kudu, and half-a-dozen other species for what today would be the trophy fee for a sable alone. But the short ranch hunts weren't the only opportunity in Rhodesia. In the outlying areas Henderson and Marsh were outfitting full-blown safaris, and in the Matetsi area both Peter Johnstone and Geoff Broom were well established.

It was about this time that I was agonizing over where to book my first African safari, so I well remember studying all the brochures and becoming totally confused. At that time South Africa was still a sleeping giant. The concept of game ranching was just getting started, and the good areas were in small pockets. Still, South Africa had her own rarities, with pioneer outfitters like Norman Deane and Basie Maartens taking hunters far and wide for vaal rhebok, nyala, and black wildebeest. It was a beginning, and by the end of the decade things were happening fast—but South Africa was not yet a real player.

South-West Africa was little different than it is today, with wonderful ranch hunting for her various species. I remember when Jack O'Connor wrote about his hunt there with Basie Maartens, and I vowed I'd go there someday. But I wanted a full-up traditional safari, and although it was tight I had saved enough money to pull it off. So I rejected all the short hunts and bargains, and I was still confused. Should I go with Ian Henderson and Brian Marsh? Should I go with Zambia Safaris? Should I go to Kenya? I know I considered Botswana, but it didn't make the final cut and I can't remember why. I was budgeted to the last dollar, and quite possibly it was a wee bit too expensive. In any case, Kenya won out. In retrospect, I'm glad it worked out that way. I didn't get the lion that was the focus of the safari, but I got a wonderful selection of East African game and, far more important, I will always carry the memory of a Kenya safari. But the truth is, in the Africa of 1977, I probably would have had a more productive safari in Zambia, Botswana, or Rhodesia. It's academic now. Professional hunter Willem van Dyk introduced me to Africa,

A fine Livingstone eland taken in Zambia's Kafue region. Zambia was closed in 2001 but is expected to reopen. The country has few outfitters and few really good concessions—but the author has been extremely lucky there.

and I loved it. We tried hard, but we didn't get a lion, which gave me an excuse to go back. But within weeks Kenya was closed, and it was no longer one of the choices.

I was back in Africa soon. Although I still desperately wanted to take a lion—and by now I knew I should hunt Zambia or Botswana—I couldn't mount another full-blown safari. But I was hooked, as anyone who visits Africa will be. I had to go back as quickly as possible, and I could afford the "new" hunting in the south.

Already things were changing. Rhodesia was in transition. Her official name was now Zimbabwe-Rhodesia, and the bush war was finally winding down. People who had thought of little but survival could start to look ahead, and hunting seemed to have a bright future. I was among the first to hunt Roger Whittall's Humani Ranch in the Lowveld, in what is today

The great Victoria Falls is located in northwestern Zimbabwe. It's easily accessible from most parts of Botswana, Zambia, and Zimbabwe—and is absolutely worth a side trip. Ed Weatherby and the author took in the falls when they hunted in Botswana in 1989.

part of the wonderful Save Valley Conservancy. Back then it was country shared by cattle and game. Ironically, only a short time previously the government hunters had finished shooting out the buffalo because of hoof-and-mouth disease, and then they made the decision to open the ranch to hunting. It would take another twenty years to return buffalo to the Save Valley!

Game ranching was still a fairly new concept in South Africa, but now it was spreading like wildfire. Bowker & Scott, Gary Kelly, Peter Knott, Coenrad Vermaak, and Norman Deane were popular outfitters in those early days. While the closure of Kenya sent clients all over southern Africa, the collapse of Mozambique particularly aided South Africa. Suddenly she was the only place to hunt nyala, and the people came. I did a short hunt for nyala with Gary Kelly's outfit near Hluhluwe, and I will never forget that I could have taken a not-yet-importable white rhino for little more than the nyala trophy fee!

The settlement of South Africa was hard on wildlife. Suddenly there was a huge demand for game, but very few properties were developed for it. The late 1970s and 1980s were a time of catching up, when prices for breeding stock soared and literally hundreds of farms converted from livestock to game. In some ways the industry grew too fast. Many fine operators sprang up, but a fair share of shady characters came along as well. Bad stories were mixed with the good, and it took time for the industry to police itself. To the credit of both the provincial governments and the Professional Hunters Association of South Africa (PHASA), they accomplished this process of weeding out in a relatively short time, though it was never completely finished.

Largely through Safari Club's efforts, CITES permits for white rhino became available in the early 1980s. When Zambia and Tanzania closed the last black rhino hunting, South Africa became the only country where the entire Big

A view across Zimbabwe's Zambezi Valley from a rocky kopje. Zimbabwe is really two safaris in one: ranch hunting in the interior, and traditional hunting in wild Africa in the border areas.

A good black lechwe taken in Zambia's Bangweulu. This is just one of dozens of southern African species and subspecies that do not occur elsewhere on the continent.

Five could be hunted. This is a proud statement for a country that, just a decade earlier, offered very limited hunting opportunities. However, neither the supply nor the demand for white rhino hunts has ever been great, and the opportunity to hunt the remainder of the Big Five remains limited in South Africa. The great opportunity in this country centers around her wealth of plains game on well-managed private lands, and the ease and low cost of the hunting. By the early 1980s South Africa had the largest safari industry on the continent, a position she still occupies in the new millennium.

The vast majority of South African safaris, numbering in the hundreds annually, are shorter hunts for several varieties of plains game. It should be noted that this type of short, inexpensive plains-game safari didn't even exist in the great days of East African hunting. Today, South Africa alone annually hosts many times the number of safaris conducted throughout East Africa in the days when the entire region was open to hunting.

After a brief transitional period, Zimbabwe-Rhodesia became Zimbabwe in 1980, and the fifteen-year bush war was over. Zimbabwe's safari industry blossomed rapidly, and, while it became commonplace for cattle ranches to be converted to game, the Zimbabwe operators didn't have to play catch-up nearly as hard as their colleagues to the south. Most of the large cattle ranches in the interior still held healthy populations of wildlife, with a variety of plains game and good numbers of leopard. Of equal importance, government and tribal lands on the periphery held large populations of elephant and buffalo and some lion. Some of these areas had been hunted during the war years. With the security problem under control, the vast Zambezi Valley to the north, the Hwange corridor to the west, and the area around Gonarezhou to the southeast could all be opened to safaris.

Zimbabwe, with the continent's second-largest safari industry, really turned into a country offering at least two

A fine herd of gemsbok in one of Namibia's grassy valleys. Namibia's game list is not extensive, but the hunting is pleasant and productive, and trophy quality is superb.

altogether different types of hunting. The first type is the ranch hunting for plains game, generally similar to the hunting in South Africa except that Zimbabwe's private ranches tend to be larger and few are game-fenced, although this is changing. The second is the longer, more traditional safari, with elephant or lion as the primary quarry. A third is a blending of the two, a safari that includes buffalo and/or leopard, perhaps combining both private land and government or tribal concessions. A much smaller country, Zimbabwe cannot host the number of safaris that her neighbor to the south can accommodate. However, she too hosts hunters in the hundreds every year, far more than Kenya ever saw in the peak of her glory.

I first hunted South-West Africa, now Namibia, back in 1979. I hunted there most recently in 1999 and have hunted several times in-between. This period has brought sweeping changes to both South Africa and Zimbabwe, but I find Namibia little changed. A big country with broad vistas,

Botswana, formerly Bechuanaland, is often called the land of the buffalo. In both the Okavango and Chobe areas, big herds are still common.

generally open country, and a human population that remains very small, this country was settled with Germanic efficiency in a grid of fairly large farms. Always a popular destination with German-speaking hunters but largely ignored by the English-speaking world, Namibia remains a fine hunting country and one of the most scenic lands in Africa. The game was very good twenty years ago, and since then game management has become more intensive, making it even better. Leopard, long hunted as vermin, now have value and are coming back. The big change was the reopening of limited elephant hunting in the north, but Namibia remains primarily a plains-game country, offering a relatively limited game list but superb trophy quality and a fine hunting experience.

Compared to South Africa, Zimbabwe, and Namibia, the safari industries in both Zambia and Botswana are small, but they are very important. These two countries, together with Tanzania, which reopened in 1981, are now just about the last and certainly the best countries offering a traditional general-bag safari that includes several members of the Big Five. Although the land and the game list vary considerably among these three countries and within their borders, safaris are conducted similarly in all three. Long gone are the days when a safari could wander at will with a mobile camp. Today the safari companies operate in finite, exclusive concessions, with camps that are more or less permanent.

Botswana has changed relatively little over the years. There has never been more than a handful of safari companies there. One drops out and another springs up, but some of the key players—like Harry Selby—have remained constant and in place since the 1960s. The hunting concessions are thus few in number but very large, now centered in either the Okavango Delta or the Chobe country to the northeast. In recent years there have been two big changes to the Botswana scene, good news and bad. The bad is that the Kalahari region, uniquely scenic and famous for big lion and gemsbok, is no longer open to hunting, although some private land opportunities have been developed. The good news is that elephant hunting has reopened. A Botswana elephant safari is extremely costly, but it offers a large population that has been undisturbed for many years. The number of elephants, coupled with relatively open country, gives Botswana the very best opportunity for elephant hunting, a status held by Zimbabwe during Botswana's long elephant closure. Game quotas in Botswana are very conservative, especially for the cats. This means trophy quality is outstanding, but Botswana safaris today tend to center around a few key trophies, and available lion permits are generally spoken for a couple of years in advance.

While Botswana has remained stable and constant, hunting in Zambia has had its ups and downs. I first hunted Zambia in 1983, and I returned in 1984. It was wonderful, but my timing was such that I barely missed some of the greatest days of Zambian hunting. Through the 1970s there were tens of thousands of elephant in the Luangwa Valley, and black rhino were still relatively common. Although ivory was generally not large, in those days it was not uncommon for a safari to take four—or even all—of the Big Five. In the late 1970s poaching gangs penetrated the Luangwa on a wholesale basis, and the great elephant herds evaporated quickly. By the time elephant and rhino closed, in the early 1980s, it was like closing the barn door after the horses were gone. Few of either species remained.

With elephant hunting closed and concessions getting shopworn, Zambia Safaris shut down in the mid-1980s. Since then Zambia has remained open, and many of the professional hunters have remained constant, but the safari companies have come and gone. As with Botswana, there has never been more than a handful of operators in this country, but, unlike Botswana, the hunting areas in Zambia have not remained constant. They have shifted back and forth from one company to another, and the areas themselves have changed. Some great hunting areas that I saw in the 1980s have been opened to settlement and are no longer hunted, or are marginal at best. On the other hand, today safaris are hunting some remote areas that simply weren't worth the trouble to get to in years gone by.

After a break of more than a decade, I returned to Zambia in 1995 and again the following year. I saw game that was wonderful by all measures—variety, numbers, and trophy quality. Human encroachment into game areas continues, but Zambia remains a fine safari country. Both the Luangwa Valley northeast of Lusaka and the Kafue region to the west are superb general-bag areas with distinct differences in species availability. In the far north the Bangweulu area is a specialized area, holding huge numbers of black lechwe and sassaby and some of Africa's best sitatunga hunting—and not much else. It is, however, a uniquely scenic area that has changed very little. Few safaris come to Zambia just to hunt Bangweulu, but it offers a worthwhile addition to any Zambia safari.

The return of South Africa's white rhino is one of conservation's greatest success stories. The white rhino has been huntable for more than twenty years, making South Africa the only country where the Big Five may be hunted today.

South Africa actually has two varieties of kudu, the southern greater kudu in the north and the Eastern Cape kudu along the southeastern coast. The latter is generally a bit smaller in the horn than the southern greater kudu but has more brilliant colors.

In the late 1980s Mozambique's long civil war finally drew to a close. Enterprising outfitters, mostly Zimbabweans like Piet Hougaard and Roger Whittall, initially reopened hunting in the Zambezi Valley corridor. At first the draw was the potential for good elephant. I hunted there with Roger Whittall in 1989, and the elephant hunting was good, but the long bush war had ravaged Mozambique's game, and there wasn't much left. Elephant hunting closed in 1990, and Whittall and his partner, Barrie Duckworth, pulled out of Mozambique. Hunting remained open. Pict Hougaard stayed and was joined by other operators, mostly from Zimbabwe and South Africa. Today there is good hunting for buffalo, cats, and a smattering of plains game in both the Zambezi Valley and along the eastern edge of Kruger National Park. Exploration continues, but so far no one has found even a small pocket that closely resembles the game paradise that was Mozambique before 1973. Regrettably, there probably isn't such a place—but Mozambique's game is rebuilding. There is viable hunting now, and with good management there is tremendous potential for the future.

Currently the countries of South Africa and Zimbabwe alone account for more than 50 percent of the safaris conducted annually across the continent. Add Namibia, Botswana, Zambia, and Mozambique, and it becomes clear that the center and lifeblood of the modern safari industry now lies in southern Africa. As we've seen, the closing of Kenya didn't start this shift, although it certainly speeded it along. It was just a quarter-century ago that I started getting serious about planning my first Africa hunt. Twenty-five years ago, when most people thought about African safari, they thought about East Africa. Photographers probably still do, but today hunters are far more likely to think about southern Africa.

In fairness—and also for the sake of accuracy and completeness—southern Africa is not the only region where hunting remains viable. In many contexts, it is not even the best. East African hunting is back in Tanzania, where a number of fine operators offer superb hunting. Tanzania is a huge and complex country, offering wonderful and very traditional general-bag hunting. The game list varies dramatically as you move from one area to another.

The total picture of African hunting hardly stops with Tanzania. Off to the west, Central African Republic and Cameroon are both important hunting countries, offering not only specialized game like bongo and Lord Derby eland but also surprisingly good general-bag hunting. Chad has reopened, and there is limited hunting in several other Central and West African countries, with much potential for further development. To the north, Ethiopia is open as well. Another giant of a country, Ethiopia deserves a far better reputation as a hunting country than it currently has. Best known as the home of the mountain nyala, Ethiopia also hosts a tremendous variety of plains game and offers very good lion hunting. The face of Africa has changed, and will continue to change, but from east to west and north to south there are great hunting opportunities. The closure of Kenya may have marked a new era, but it was not the end of African hunting.

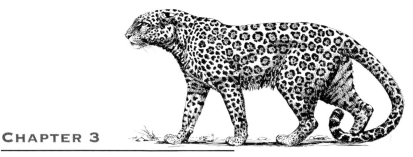

CHAPTER 3

THE SAFARI INDUSTRY TODAY

Africa is a troubled continent, but she remains a hunter's paradise.

One's first African experience seems to elicit universal responses that are strange yet consistent. A first-time parachutist or scuba diver usually doesn't consider himself or herself an expert at the sport, but the first-time African hunter almost invariably comes home an expert on all things African. It is common for the first-time hunter to speak and write authoritatively and expansively about his or her experiences. I did it myself! Those in the audience who have genuine African experience are usually amused, but the inexperienced are likely to take such a limited viewpoint as gospel. Africa does offer a truly marvelous experience, and the intensity of the first safari is such that it is almost always a pivotal experience in one's life, an unforgettable episode that can never quite be relived. One's first professional hunter is almost certain to be the greatest of heroes, and the first country or area almost certain to be the most legendary of all game areas. Maybe the professional hunter was really that good, and maybe the area was really that good . . . but what is the basis for such a comparison?

Usually there is little harm in the pontification of a first-time African hunter, and professional hunters benefit immensely from the enthusiasm of new clients. From a pragmatic standpoint, however, it's always best to take such impressions with a grain of salt. One predictable statement that I find harmful is the prophesying of gloom and doom

There remains a great deal of wonderful hunting country in Africa, but today's operators are often hunting areas that, twenty years ago, would have been too much trouble to reach.

for the future of African hunting. Clear back in 1909 Roosevelt expressed misgivings about the future of African wildlife—this when he was literally creating the concept of safari as we now know it. Hemingway did it in the thirties and Ruark did it in the fifties, and yet African hunting and the safari industry remain vibrant and vital. No, not the same, never the same . . . but still wonderful and still a proper and possible dream for any hunter.

From my first African safari (when I knew much less than I thought I did) until today (when I'm still learning), I have written a great deal about Africa. As I have mentioned, my own African experience started in Kenya, shortly before Kenya closed and when the safari industry was at its nadir. It seemed the doomsayers were right, that African hunting was on its way out. I hope that I have never contributed to this legacy of negativism. Certainly I have tried to avoid the temptation, but I must admit that I bought into it in my own safari planning!

Just a decade ago most of us thought elephant hunting was nearly over. Today the animals and the hunting opportunities are increasing, and will continue to increase. In Zimbabwe, where this jumbo was taken, meat and hide recovery has progressed to a fine art, with nothing going to waste.

Secretly believing that African hunting was dying, during the past twenty years I have indulged my African passion to an obsessive degree. I count more than forty separate hunts (many of them back-to-back) in a dozen different countries. This is far more African hunting than I can realistically afford and, as a gunwriter and hunting writer, far more than I can ever write about. Now that the millennium has turned, I see that there was little reason for such haste.

As we have seen, the great days of East African hunting are gone, but much great hunting remains. Countries are open now that were not open then. Back in '89 I was in a great hurry to get a decent tusker, for fear all elephant hunting would be history. Now we can see that we have turned that corner. The days of the hundred-pound tuskers are pretty much over, but elephant are on the increase in many countries. Opportunity today is better than it has been since the mid-1980s and will continue to improve. At this writing, all of the principal spiral-horned antelope can be readily hunted, which certainly was not always the case. Black rhino hunting is a thing of the past, but hunting for the rest of the traditional Big Five, plus white rhino, is secure.

I do not regret my longtime immersion in African hunting, but I might have taken things at a more leisurely pace. As I reach middle age I find the mountains are growing steeper; I might have put off a few flat-country African hunts in favor of some sheep hunts I might have done when they were not only physically easier but also more affordable. We all have choices to make, and there was a time when I could have chosen to hunt desert sheep or polar bear at a small fraction of today's cost. To this day I count neither of these important animals among my life's experience, but I have hunted several times in each of the relatively costly safari countries such as Botswana, C.A.R., Tanzania, and Zambia!

Africa has her problems. Few countries are truly stable in the way the western world thinks of political stability. Over the next few years I am certain that some countries now open to hunting will close, and some now closed will open. The players will change, but there will be African hunting as long as there are African hunters, simply because the economic viability of an organized and regulated safari industry is too attractive for it to be otherwise. But this view does not apply in every locale. The great threat to African wildlife and African hunting is not politics but human encroachment. Wildlife habitat is being lost to agriculture, ranching, and other human development at an alarming rate. Although the worldwide ban on ivory trade has greatly reduced elephant poaching across the continent, meat poaching is an ever-escalating threat as the number of hungry people increases. Some remote areas have become virtual wasteland, and there is little money and apparently even less incentive to do anything about it. Countries with extremely active safari industries will be able to set aside land for wildlife, and have found it in their best interests to maintain active anti-poaching measures. Programs such as Zimbabwe's CAMPFIRE and Zambia's ADMADE, which allow local villages to share directly in concession and trophy fees from safaris, have made tremendous progress in promoting the concept of wildlife coexisting with man. As Africa's human population continues to increase, such programs are ever more essential. But ultimately they might not be enough, because there is only so much land.

In the short term I envision few sweeping changes to safari hunting as it is today. The old Africa, where wildlife roams freely and lions still roar, will continue to shrink gradually, but intensive wildlife management on private lands will continue and will gradually increase. One day, I fear, private land will offer the only viable hunting remaining in Africa— but that day is many years away, and the change will continue to be gradual. One very real risk, however, is that a number of countries currently open to hunting will have very small safari industries, with just a handful of outfitters.

Regardless of the local traditions, it comes down to economics and politics. Zimbabwe, South Africa, and Namibia, with huge and economically vital safari industries, are firmly entrenched as hunting countries. Botswana, Zambia, Ethiopia, Central African Republic, and Cameroon are hunting countries with viable safari industries, but the number of outfitters and thus the overall economic impact is very small. They will remain open so long as there is no compelling reason for things to be otherwise, but in my opinion there are no guarantees. Tanzania is a special case. She has a large and economically significant hunting industry and also a huge landmass that can support a large number of safaris. But she has previously experimented with a hunting closure (1973 to 1981); she has continuing difficulties with allocation of hunting areas; and she has experienced scandals with unscrupulous operators, which have rocked her safari industry, her government, and the international hunting community. I think Tanzania will remain a hunting country, but I wouldn't stake my life on it.

The players will change, but there will be African hunting for many years to come. It will not be the same, but it will be wonderful and there will be choices. Unlike much of the world's great hunting, most African hunting can be enjoyed by hunters well past their middle years. No, I don't regret pushing as hard as I have to see as much of Africa as I could, but I don't think it was necessary to hurry. Roosevelt's Africa is gone. So is Hemingway's, and Ruark's, and even Peter Capstick's. Change will continue. But if I'm still able to follow buffalo tracks thirty years from now, I believe there will be tracks to follow. And young hunters just starting out should not fear there will be no African hunting when they are financially able to go. Unfortunately, it is impossible to predict exactly what countries will be available in thirty, twenty, or even ten years from now. But I can give a brief rundown on the African scene today, and some thoughts on what the future might hold.

CORE HUNTING COUNTRIES

In terms of numbers of operators and numbers of safaris, today's safari industry centers around South Africa, Zimbabwe, and Namibia. In my view the countries of Botswana, Tanzania, and Zambia are also of critical importance because they form the backbone of the traditional general-bag safari. Each has a selection of highly desirable plains species, including two or more of the Big Five on the normal safari. In terms of numbers of safaris, the countries of Cameroon, Central African Republic, and Ethiopia are not significant. Even so, I consider all three essential "core" hunting countries because, among many desirable trophies, each holds important species that are of primary importance to serious African hunters: bongo and Lord Derby eland in Cameroon and C.A.R.; mountain nyala in Ethiopia. So, with apologies to those who don't agree with my list, here's a brief rundown on my concept of today's core hunting countries.

BOTSWANA

Botswana offers prime general-bag hunting, with some of Africa's best lion hunting, good leopard, plenty of buffalo, and one of the last opportunities to hunt elephant as part of a general-bag safari rather than as a specialized pursuit. There is a good selection of plains game, including good sable, greater kudu, sitatunga, and red lechwe. The safari industry here is generally hampered by very limited game quotas. (*Read:* When booking Botswana safaris, be very specific about desired game.) Most hunting today is in the Okavango region and the Chobe region. Significant game management on private lands is just getting off the ground.

CAMEROON

This is a land of two types of safaris: specialized forest hunting for bongo and other forest game in the south, and savanna hunting for Lord Derby eland, roan, and a goodly selection of other species in the north. There are relatively few outfitters, with most hunting concentrating on bongo. However, elephant hunting is open, and there are both lion and buffalo in most northern concessions. There is much meat poaching in the hinterlands, which is a great, ongoing concern. The politics (and the politics of hunting) are shaky throughout Central and West Africa, so the future is uncertain; but Cameroon offers excellent hunting.

CENTRAL AFRICAN REPUBLIC

The same can be said for C.A.R. as for Cameroon, except that C.A.R. is far better for Lord Derby eland, while Cameroon is better for western roan. Incursions of organized meat

In terms of numbers of safaris, neither Cameroon nor C.A.R. can touch the southern countries. Even so, both are extremely important because they offer the best hunting for several important species. PH Jacques Lemaux and Joe Bishop pose with a wonderful Lord Derby eland taken in northeastern C.A.R.

poachers from Sudan have severely reduced the game along C.A.R.'s eastern border. However, C.A.R. is a very large country with a small human population, and although the safari industry is not large, the government appears committed to maintaining a sport-hunting industry.

ETHIOPIA

This huge country has tremendous potential and an extremely extensive game list. However, a handful of licensed professional hunters host a very small number of safaris annually. The only country where mountain nyala may be found, Ethiopia also offers superb hunting for a wide variety of species in the Omo Valley

Ethiopia is best known as the only place to hunt mountain nyala, and for this reason the author considers her a "core country." Unfortunately, many overlook the fact that Ethiopia also holds wonderful general-bag hunting. This fine beisa oryx was taken in the Danakil.

to the south and Danakil to the north. Hunting has been on-again, off-again for many years, but a newly instituted program of exclusive concessions and game quotas suggests government commitment to a hunting program. There is a bright future, but only if Ethiopia can sell her safaris on the world market.

NAMIBIA

Often overlooked by Americans but a favorite among Europeans, Namibian hunting is stable and well organized and offers some of Africa's most beautiful scenery. Hunting is also very economical. This country offers Africa's best gemsbok, good kudu, and a good selection of other plains game. There is limited elephant hunting in the north. Leopard hunting is difficult but is generally increasing.

SOUTH AFRICA

In this country, Africa's largest safari industry currently hosts the largest number of safaris. Hunting is well-organized, exceptionally productive, and generally economical—all primarily because most hunting is conducted on well-managed private lands. There is a huge selection of plains game, including numerous indigenous rarities such as vaal rhebok, nyala, blesbok, bontebok, black wildebeest, and more. South Africa also offers *limited* hunting for the entire Big Five. Lion, buffalo, and elephant are generally hunted along the Kruger Park corridor. Due to increased protection and economic value, leopard are increasing in many areas. White rhino are usually found in small herds on private lands. The safari industry is huge and economically critical to South Africa, but rising crime and South Africa's current move toward stringent gun control pose serious concerns for the industry's future.

TANZANIA

This huge country hosts numerous safari operators. It is perhaps the most traditional general-bag safari country, aided by government-mandated twenty-one-day minimums for most important antelope species. The game list varies dramatically by region. The northern region (Masailand) hosts East African species; the central and western regions (Rungwa and westward) hold southern species such as sable and roan; and the southeast, with the great Selous Reserve, offers excellent (and improving) elephant hunting and a good selection of other game. Virtually all areas offer buffalo, lion, and leopard in varying densities. The Tanzanian government has been embarrassed by some shenanigans by unscrupulous outfitters,

South Africa is blessed with a wealth of species and subspecies that cannot be found or hunted anywhere else. To my mind, one of her top prizes is the elusive little vaal rhebok, one of Africa's few genuine mountain species.

With most safaris limited in both duration and objectives, the true "general-bag" safari is a rarity today. This was a week's bag from Zambia's Mulobezi area in 1996—an incredible run of luck for a modern safari.

but the economic impact of hunting is important enough that the future should be secure, if not for all outfitters in all areas.

ZAMBIA

Zambia is a superb general-bag country, with excellent lion and leopard hunting (though not in all concessions), good buffalo, and a fine selection of common antelope and local rarities. Africa's best sable, good southern roan, Kafue and black lechwe, and fine sitatunga are among the highlights, but the game list and quality of hunting do vary significantly from one area to another. The safari industry is small, and Zambia's outfitters come and go, but on the whole Zambia, open for hunting continuously since independence in 1964, appears committed to remaining a hunting country.

ZIMBABWE

Zimbabwe holds Africa's second-largest safari industry, next to South Africa. It offers essentially two different safaris in one country: in the interior, exceptional plains-game hunting on large, well-developed private lands; on the borders, traditional hunting for buffalo, elephant, and lion. Leopard are endemic throughout Zimbabwe, but lion hunting is generally poor (with some significant exceptions). Zimbabwe offers some of the best and most economical hunting for buffalo, elephant, and leopard; it also offers superb hunting for a wide variety of plains game, including Africa's best greater kudu. The safari industry is extremely stable and of great economic importance to Zimbabwe.

OTHER OPPORTUNITIES

The nine countries listed above are not the only countries currently open to hunting. Depending on the species sought, they may not even be the best, although in my opinion they

There are still many fine buffalo areas in Africa, but Zimbabwe offers the simplest and most economical buffalo hunting on today's market. Swarovski's Jim Morey took this bull in Russ Broom's area on a short hunt in 1999.

are the most important and most visible. Scattered across the continent, numerous other countries are also open, generally for limited species or in limited areas. These come and go as the political winds change, but several are worthy of mention.

Congo is now open and offers superb forest hunting. It has wonderful potential for bongo and is perhaps the best area for dwarf buffalo and forest sitatunga. In the Red Sea Hills of northern Sudan, Angelo Dacey continues to offer Nubian ibex hunting and other game. The security situation varies and the wildlife has been heavily poached, but continued hunting in the north offers hope that hunting will someday resume in southern Sudan. After decades of civil war, Chad is now reopened on a limited basis. The great general-bag hunting along the Aouk River may never return, but veteran PH Alain Lefol has uncovered pockets of western greater kudu and native-range aoudad, among other species. Mozambique has been reopened since the late 1980s, with several outfitters now offering good hunting for buffalo and some hunting for lion, leopard, and a smattering of plains game. Mozambique's game is definitely increasing, and the potential is superb. Unfortunately, her wildlife was so badly ravaged during the long bush war that it will take many more years before she can be the safari country she was in the early 1970s.

Quite a lot of hunting is scattered here and there in the great bulge of West Africa, but the status of hunting in these countries seems to be in flux. Burkina Faso has a small but stable hunting program for western roan and other species. Neighboring Benin has had some on-and-off hunting for similar species, and the same potential exists in Mali and Togo. Senegal has long been open for limited species. Popular among French hunters, Senegal is another good place for economical western roan. Down in the forest zone, Liberia is reopening and should offer excellent hunting for a wide variety of forest duikers, important to serious trophy collectors.

NOT MUCH HOPE

Humans being basically optimistic creatures, and also of a nostalgic bent, it has long been in fashion to speculate about the wonderful hunting that would be available if we could just get one or another of the "old countries" reopened. I used to follow that line of thinking, but I've seen too much of Africa to believe in hidden hot spots awaiting discovery. The only place where African wildlife remains plentiful is where that wildlife has been protected. And the Third World reality is that wildlife has been protected only in the places where it has economic viability. In ravaged countries like Uganda and Somalia, there is virtually no hope for wildlife, whether hunted or not. Kenya has excellent wildlife in her national parks, but little else remains except on some large private lands. There has been speculation that Kenya would reopen since the very day she closed, but I don't think it much matters anymore. Some years ago Malawi was opened very briefly, and she has some pockets of excellent nyala and a little of this and that, including some elephant, but, in reality, she has neither the variety nor the density for a genuine safari industry.

MAYBE AGAIN SOMEDAY . . .

Having said that I don't believe in fairy tales, I cannot bring myself to give up hope altogether that certain areas will come back. Angola now holds the record for Africa's longest-running bush war, and the destruction must be almost total. She is a huge country, however, and maybe the war has bypassed pockets somewhere. The recent discovery of a small population of giant sable does give hope. I personally have seen what poachers from Sudan have done to eastern C.A.R., and this suggests there must be very little wildlife remaining on the Sudanese side of the border. Even so, the country is so huge and the wildlife resources were formerly so vast that surely something must remain. I doubt there is much, but perhaps somewhere in the depths of the great Sudd there are still Nile lechwe, and in the transition forest the bongo will be the very last to succumb to poachers.

Without question there is great potential in Zaire, not necessarily because of any game management but simply because the forest is still so huge in this giant country. She has been open in recent years, offering wonderful bongo hunting that closed due to purely political considerations. And now that elephant poaching has been greatly reduced, it is almost certain that somewhere in Zaire's forests lurk some of the continent's greatest remaining tuskers.

The potential for desert hunting remains a subject for speculation. Despite the rumors, it is almost certain that both scimitar-horned oryx and addax are extinct or nearly so, and even if any remain, they certainly will not be hunted for sport. However, there are viable populations of Nubian ibex, aoudad, and gazelle scattered across North Africa. Egypt still has a moratorium on hunting. She has quite good potential for Nubian ibex and gazelle. Indeed, Nubian ibex extend through the Sinai Peninsula and into Israel, so there is much potential for hunting if peaceful times ever come. Morocco has done a good job rebuilding her herds of aoudad, and fully a decade ago it seemed certain a hunting program would open. It never happened, but the aoudad are still there, so hope remains.

No, I don't believe in fairy tales, and I am certain that Hemingway's green hills are gone forever, not simply awaiting rediscovery. But Africa is such a vast and complex continent that it defies generalizations. At this writing at least fifteen countries are officially open to hunting—as many as there have been at any time in the last hundred years. By the time you read these lines the list may have changed slightly, and it will change still more with the passage of years. But there is fine hunting now, and great hope for the future.

THE MODERN PROFESSIONAL HUNTER

Sadly, he has become as much a businessman as a hunter, a truck driver as much a tracker, and a charmer as much as a man of action. Perhaps this is unavoidable, for the modern safari is big business. To be successful the PH must sell his safaris and charm his clients, and also be astute enough as a businessman to show a profit at year's end. That said, I am increasingly concerned about the genuine qualifications of many PHs in the field today. Some countries, like Zimbabwe, require formal apprenticeship and a passing grade on both written and practical exams. At the other extreme, there are still countries where an unqualified outsider can bribe his or her way into a professional hunter's license.

The current trend, almost continent-wide, is to increasingly restrict issuance of licenses to local citizens, or to simply deny work permits to outsiders. This is not altogether a bad thing, because it prevents unqualified folks from buying their way in. On the other hand, it's not altogether a good thing, because local hunters may not always be properly qualified, and extremely competent PHs from elsewhere in Africa may not be able to ply their trade.

I believe very strongly in properly qualified professional hunters. Not only does a good professional hunter enhance the African experience, but you literally place your life in your PH's hands. You want those hands to be qualified and competent.

My personal bias has always been in favor of African-born PHs. Mind you, some Americans and Europeans have done extremely well; just being born in Nairobi or Johannesburg is not a qualification! How do you know if you have a good PH? First, remember that most outfitters use multiple PHs. Never book a safari without knowing who the professional hunter will be, and never accept the booking without checking references on that PH. You are always within your rights to ask to see a

The biggest threat to African hunting today is shrinking habitat due to rapidly increasing human populations. More and more habitat is being lost to grazing and subsistence farming, and few areas remain that have no villages.

professional hunter's license, but even today the licensing system is "squishy" enough in many countries that it may not tell you what you need to know. More important, your PH should belong to the local professional hunter's association and to the International Professional Hunters Association (IPHA). The latter membership requires the recommendation of several clients, so the most promising beginner in the world may not have it. Those who are members should be OK.

HOW SAFE ARE SAFARIS?

I can't tell you and won't attempt to. Most hunting areas are safer than your own backyard, and most African cities are, at worst, only slightly less safe than any large American city. Having been in some areas that were purported to be dangerous, my opinion is that our press tends to sensationalize the negative. On the other hand, hunting is supposed to be fun, and only an idiot would knowingly take a safari into a war zone. What competent and ethical professional hunter would take his client into an unsafe area? Read the newspapers, pay attention to State Department warnings, and listen to your own instincts, but book your PH based on references and reputation, and trust him. You're trusting a lot of dollars to him, and you may be trusting your life to his coolness with dangerous game. Trust him to choice of hunting area as well. If things get dicey in a given area, he is far more likely to offer a switch to Plan B than to return a deposit that is most likely long since spent; but he does not, under any circumstances, want his clients to be in an unnecessarily dangerous situation. That just ain't the way the modern safari industry works!

PART II

THE COUNTRY
AND THE GAME

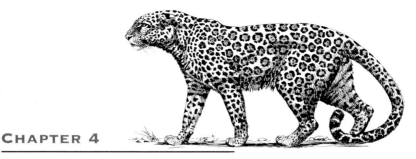

CHAPTER 4

AFRICAN GAME COUNTRY

Africa is blessed with the greatest diversity of wildlife on earth, and her game is found in almost every type of habitat. What does African game country look like? That depends on where you are!

Some of us were stricken by the African bug early in life, while it came late to others. Regardless of when it hit, most people reading these lines have a burning desire to go to Africa, or to go back again. This is as it should be; Africa is indeed the stuff dreams are made of, and no matter how hard we try, none of us will ever see enough of her. But those dreams of Africa have to come from somewhere, and for most of us they had their beginnings in books or films. The lore and legend of African hunting has spawned some of the very best sporting books, and there are a few very good "safari" films and videos.

Certainly I recommend reading as much as you can prior to a first safari, and continuing to read while sitting out the long months until the next safari. Films are useful as well. But there are pitfalls to both media. Africa is a huge continent, so large that the United States can fit onto the map of Africa some half-dozen times. It stands to reason that a landmass so huge would have a great diversity of topography and vegetation, and indeed Africa does. When starting to dream of Africa, hunters of my generation were likely to imagine Tarzan's jungles, which Hollywood created in southern California. Hunters of today are more likely to imagine the sweeping panoramas of *Out of Africa* or the grassy plains of *Ghost and the Darkness*.

Both stereotypical habitats do exist, but you might not see either of them on your safari. Come to think of it, there is actually very little true canopy jungle in Africa, but there are vast climax forests and huge expanses of savanna grassland. There are also high mountains, great swamps, huge deserts, and thousands upon thousands of miles of thornbush. What you can expect to encounter depends upon exactly where you go in this vast continent.

We could discuss the hunting countries, one by one, and describe the types of habitat within them; or we could discuss the major habitat types and the regions in which they occur. Either is a daunting task in a continent as large as Africa. We will follow the latter course, because there are no absolutes. All African hunting countries offer several types of habitat, if only in limited areas, and some countries offer every type. In my mind I divide African game country into desert, mountain, swamp, savanna, forest, and thornbush—understanding this is a gross oversimplification. There are usually gradations as you move from one type to another, and there are also anomalies. For instance, while it's appropriate to think of the forest zone as very thick country where shooting will be at short range, scattered throughout are natural grassy clearings and swampy areas where shooting can be very far indeed. Africa's mountains can be up-and-down forest or thornbush, or they can be open grassy slopes. Stay with me and see if we can make sense of this huge and diverse continent.

DESERT

With the possible exceptions of northern Sudan and the north of newly reopened Chad, there is now virtually no hunting in the true Sahara-like desert of endless sands. Even historically, most of the Sahara Desert safaris were conducted amid the desert grasses and low shrubs along the great desert's southern fringes. This is consistent with desert hunting elsewhere on the continent. The Danakil of Ethiopia; Kenya's northern frontier district; the Kalahari of Botswana, Namibia, and South Africa; Namibia's Namib; and South Africa's Great Karroo are all considered living deserts. Groundwater (unless developed by man) is scarce, but plant life is abundant.

While the sand dunes of the Namib and some parts of the Kalahari are spectacular, these areas are more properly characterized by low shrubs, grasses, and occasional stunted but extremely hardy trees. Many of these plants offer exceptionally high food value, and of course the desert springs to life when the infrequent rain arrives. Desert wildlife generally consists of two groups: migrating animals that follow the rain and are present only when there has been rainfall, and animals that have adapted to arid conditions. The former group includes herd animals such as wildebeest and elephant; the latter group includes oryx and gazelle.

MOUNTAINS

Africa holds very little of the alpine habitat that most sheep hunters think of, but she does have a surprising amount of high country. There are arid desert mountains in Chad, northern C.A.R., and northern Sudan, not to mention the rugged Atlas Mountains of North Africa. The spine of Ethiopia is an extremely high plateau, with mountain ranges such as the Arusis, the Din Dins, and the Cherchers rising to as high as twelve thousand feet. However, because of the equatorial climate you won't find rocky peaks and open basins up there; instead you will find the tops generally covered with thick heather.

Most of Masailand is also a high plateau, often six thousand feet in elevation, but instead of ranges of mountains the land rises in widely separated individual mountains. Two of these are Mount Kilimanjaro and Mount Meru, but there are many of lesser prominence. While Masailand is a mixture of savanna and thornbush, most of the mountains are characterized by lush vegetation that can be as thick as any jungle Tarzan ever saw.

Several distinct varieties of mountain reedbuck occur discontinuously from Ethiopia to South Africa. This is a Chanler mountain reedbuck taken in Tanzania.

Elsewhere there are lush highlands, and most areas boast high hills and the typical rocky kopjes, but you have to go pretty far south to run into more real mountains. In South Africa there are real mountains, and lots of them. The Drakensbergs are a rugged, high spine extending south and west from Natal. Farther south the Cape Mountains rise abruptly from the Indian Ocean coastline. In both cases you may glass for game amid rocky ridges that look a lot like Wyoming and Montana along the Rocky Mountain front. It is downright shocking to get snowed on while hunting the Cape Mountains in winter, but it's not unusual. Farther west, Namibia's Orongo Mountains form another rocky, arid spine that always reminds me of Arizona's Coues deer mountains.

Africa has a few genuine mountain species. The aoudad, the Nubian ibex and the long-protected walia ibex, and Ethiopia's mountain nyala are among them. There are also

The sitatunga is probably the most important game animal in Africa's swamps. Usually found near papyrus reed beds, the sitatunga occurs discontinuously from West Africa to Botswana and Angola.

varieties of mountain reedbuck and mountain zebra, and localized mountain species such as vaal rhebok and klipspringer. The specialized mountain game is always interesting, but even where these species do not occur, Africa's mountains usually hold interesting game. The lush, thick high country often forms its own ecosystem above the valleys and plains, and it is there that you often find the biggest leopard and buffalo, and it is there that you might look for a big bushbuck or greater kudu.

SWAMPS

In general, Africa's seasons are not a matter of heat and cold but of rain and dry. Permanent wetlands of vast papyrus reed beds and pools covered with lily pads surround many of Africa's lakes and rivers and estuaries. There are also vast areas that flood during the rains but gradually dry out during the long, dry months that follow the rainy season. Most African rivers have these flood plains, and they can extend for miles. They are virtually swamps during the rainy season and for several weeks after it; but in the dry season they appear as vast, flat, short-grass plains. As the water recedes, so does the area we would call a swamp, until all that remains are the reed beds and pools close to the major river or body of water that causes the flooding.

Most African countries, from the watershed of the Nile south to the Limpopo, have swamps and flood plains, and some of them ring as great names in African game country. The great Sudd, from which Sudan takes its name, is such a place, as are the Kafue Flats and Bangweulu of Zambia. Probably the most famous is Botswana's Okavango, properly not a swamp but an inland delta. The Okavango River flows down out of Angola, and not far from Maun it divides into dozens of clear-flowing channels separated by innumerable palm-studded islands. Farther south the river comes back together again, then flows out into the Kalahari and vanishes, truly one of the great wonders of the world. Consistent with other African wetlands, during the rains the Okavango extends far out into the surrounding savanna and thornbush; during the dry season, it recedes into the network of channels and palm islands.

As with the mountains, there are relatively few game species that are true swamp dwellers. Principal among them are the varieties of sitatunga and lechwe, and crocodile and hippo are endemic. The wetlands are often favored hideouts for buffalo and elephant, and the surrounding areas just beyond the water's edge are usually rich with a tremendous variety of wildlife.

SAVANNA

As there are differences in the height of mountains and the depth of swamps, there are different kinds of savannas.

When I think of true savanna I think of broad, grassy plains, the classic Serengeti habitat. The reality is that truly large plains exist in relatively few areas that are being hunted today. Kenya had a lot of open country, and the plains of *Out of Africa* flow on south to Tanzania. Most of Masailand is a high, grassy plateau with wooded hills and watercourses, with the Serengeti off to the west—but Tanzania is a huge country, and these classic East African savannas do not constitute a large percentage of the total landmass. Much of Ethiopia's Danakil is true short-grass savanna, as is the famed Aouk River country in southern Chad and northern C.A.R., extending west to extreme northern Cameroon. In South Africa, much of the Orange Free State and the approaches to both the Karroo and the Kalahari are broad, grassy plains, and the same can be said of much of central and southern Namibia.

Even in these areas there are few places where the plains extend from horizon to horizon. More often grassland is interspersed with fingers of thornbush and woodland—what you might call savanna woodland. And on the northern fringes of Central Africa's forest zone, there is just the opposite effect, with fingers of savanna extending deep into the trees. As you might expect, the primary species in true savanna are the grazers. This is where you will find wildebeest, hartebeest, and zebra—sometimes in the thousands. Where there is adequate cover to lie up in during the heat of the day, you will find buffalo as well, and of course you will find the great cats following the herbivores.

FOREST

Africa's forest zone is a huge expanse of country extending across Zaire west to the Atlantic; north to southern Sudan, C.A.R., and Cameroon; and on west across the bulge of West Africa. As discussed in a previous chapter, there is currently

The forests of Central Africa are beautiful when you can see them from a distance. Up close, this is a very difficult area to hunt!

The forest zone is technically not a jungle but a climax forest of tall trees, underbrush, and minimum visibility. Typically you see little game, but some of Africa's great prizes dwell in the forest.

relatively little hunting in the forest zone, considering its huge size. However, this is primarily a matter of current politics rather than availability of wildlife resources. Right now southern C.A.R. and Cameroon are the most important hunting areas in the forest. Limited hunting in Congo and Liberia is just now reopening. Compared to other places on the continent, the number of safaris into the forest zone annually is very small, but the game is important enough that most serious hunters eventually make at least one forest safari.

The forest is different from all the rest. It is not a jungle; the African forest is a true tall-tree climax forest of huge mahogany and many other species. The underbrush is generally thick—so thick that a human will spend much of his day walking doubled over or crawling to get underneath the lattice of vines and thorny branches. This, by the way, is probably the most difficult part of forest hunting. The walking is slow, because, whether on tracks or not, you might see game at any moment. Even in the hottest months the heat is not brutal, because you are walking in constant and permanent shade. But the constant bending over is hard on most hunters.

Where there are still lots of elephant, their broad trails make traversing the forest a walk in the park. Unfortunately, elephant in the more accessible—and most often hunted—northern fringes of the forest were badly hammered during the days of heavy poaching in the 1970s and 1980s. They are starting to rebuild, but the reduction was so dramatic that many former elephant roads are now simply overgrown tangles.

Even though the vegetation is so thick that visibility is most often measured in feet, there is little good browsing or grazing on the forest floor (which is typical of climax forest everywhere). Such conditions mean that game is thinly distributed. To compound the relative scarcity of game, the hunter must overcome the animal's superior nose, eyes, and ears to get very close before the game is in view. To me the most difficult thing about forest hunting is that you can, quite literally, go days and days without seeing anything beyond birds and monkeys.

And yet the forest game is both diverse and fascinating. There are still a lot of elephant in the depths of the forest. There are true forest buffalo and, on the northern fringes, buffalo that are a transition between the red forest variety and the black Cape or southern varieties. There are some leopard, some bushbuck, and some warthogs and bushpigs. There are also the specialized forest species. Principal is the bongo, the African hunter's Holy Grail—but one mustn't overlook the giant forest hog, the forest races of sitatunga, and the incredible diversity of forest duikers. The forest is a different and difficult world, especially after one has viewed the abundance of wildlife in most African areas.

Hunting techniques in the forest are limited: One can spoor with or without dogs, or wait over a small clearing or natural salt lick. Either requires great patience and mental discipline. I have never been physically challenged in the forest, but mentally it is the most difficult hunting I have ever done. It is best suited to the experienced African hunter who knows what he or she is in for. The trade-off is not only some of the continent's most prized game but a chance to see chimpanzee and gorilla and walk through the uniquely beautiful and fascinating realm of the world's greatest forest.

THORNBUSH AND WOODLAND

This is a catchall for the most prevalent habitat type in African game country today—a mixture of thorny shrubs and smallish hardwoods that limits visibility to a couple of hundred yards, depending on the time of year. Beyond the high-water mark, most African swamps are surrounded by thornbush. Most true savannas are cut by watercourses lined with thick

The greater kudu is one of Africa's most widespread species, occurring discontinuously from the Cape to Chad. Although highly adaptable, the kudu is a browser most frequently found in thornbush and woodland.

The baobab or cream of tartar tree is widespread in African woodlands, and, though it doesn't precisely describe a habitat type, it is one of the most distinctive sights in Africa.

riverine growth. Most hills and mountains are covered with heavy bush, and even the huntable portions of African deserts often look more like thin thornbush than true savanna.

I am not an expert on African flora and will not pretend to be. However, there are a number of African trees that are as descriptive of Africa as her unique wildlife—and some of them virtually define the habitat type. The flat-topped acacia, of which there are many species, is classic of Africa. The acacia is a hardy tree requiring little water, and it is generally seen in plains country, often standing alone. Equally recognizable is the baobab, also widely distributed. It usually rises in a woodland dominated by other species but is always recognizable by its size and unusual shape. The trees that dominate African game country are not nearly so recognizable, but their presence literally describes the country.

African game habitat extends from northern South Africa and Mozambique through Zimbabwe, Zambia, eastern Botswana, and western Tanzania, skirting the eastern plains and coastal bush and the great central forests and continuing north to the fringes of the Sahara. Most of this habitat is a mixture of thorny shrubs and hardwoods in varying density. To the casual observer the vegetation across this tremendous span of Africa actually looks quite similar, but in this mixture of underbrush, saplings, and mature trees, the dominant plant varies considerably with the soil, climate, and local rainfall. The mix of vegetation also varies.

From the Limpopo drainage north to the Zambezi, most of the country is mopane woodland, the mopane being a deciduous hardwood somewhat resembling oak but of limited size. Farther north, across most of Zambia and western Tanzania, the soil is more sandy, and the mopanes give way to Brachystegia, another hardwood that defines the *miombo* forest. Because of the poorer soil, this type of forest generally offers somewhat better visibility than the typically heavy underbrush of mopane forest. In

Today perhaps the majority of African hunting is done in fairly thick thornbush. This is typical mopane forest, a hardwood forest with thick undergrowth, in Zimbabwe.

Tanzania you begin to see more Terminalia, another family of hardwood with numerous varieties. Farther north, between the forest zone and the grasslands below the Sahara, Terminalia is the dominant tree, and the country is often described as Terminalia woodland. Fortunately, this woodland has a healthy sprinkling of the leafy *Isoberlinia doka* favored by giant eland. Grazing animals use the woodlands for security cover but feed in the openings; properly, the woodlands are home to the browsing animals, with the various races of greater kudu and eland occurring literally from north to south.

Whether in central Cameroon or in the Transvaal, this mosaic of African woodland and thornbush is characterized by limited visibility. This country is not nearly as dense as forest, but the cycle of the deciduous plants has a great impact on how far you can see and thus how you must hunt. (Visibility varies with the season; remember that the Terminalia forests of Central Africa are above the equator, while most *miombo* and mopane forests have opposite seasons.) Before the leaves fall, visibility beyond

The plains we all saw in Out of Africa *do exist—but not in many areas. This is the Great Rift Valley in Tanzania's Masailand.*

one hundred yards is unusual; with the leaves gone, experienced hunters can often see game through the trees at two or three times that distance. There are natural clearings throughout this vast region, some of them quite large. Most areas have at least some hills that offer vantage points down into a valley or across to the next hill, and the density of the vegetation differs. The thick *jess* of southern Africa's riverine habitat is as thick as anything you will see in the forest, and some woodlands are very open and might properly be called savanna woodland.

It is thus an oversimplification to say that shooting in thornbush/woodland country is usually on the order of 75 to 150 yards. That's a true statement, but occasionally there's an opportunity for a longer shot—and, just as occasionally, you may have to crawl within bayonet range to even see the game you are spooring. This kind of country calls for the greatest versatility in terms of rifles and hunting technique. In the forest, you can almost be sure the shots will be very close; in savanna, desert, swamp, and mountain habitats most shots will

71

be longish, as African hunting goes. In the forest, riflescopes and binoculars are of limited utility; in the plains, swamps, deserts, and mountains you must have good binoculars, and without a scope your shooting options are very limited. In thornbush, anything can happen. In the morning you may track buffalo in the thick *jess*, but you might spend the afternoon glassing a deep canyon.

Throughout Africa you are likely to encounter a variety of these habitat types in one safari, and sometimes on the same day. In Masailand you may hunt the hills for kudu and such in the morning, and hunt gazelle on the plains in the afternoon; in Botswana you may hunt thornbush and savanna for wildebeest in the morning and glass papyrus reed beds for sitatunga in the afternoon. Even in the forest, you may track bongo in the morning and watch a clearing for yellowback duiker in the afternoon. Even within a given area the country changes, and so does the game. Some species are specific to one habitat type; others may be found almost anywhere, depending on current food sources and external forces such as hunting pressure. You could say that Zimbabwe is characterized by thick woodland, while the Serengeti is open plains. In both cases you would be basically right—but there are few absolutes. In the following few chapters we will look at African game, with an eye to understanding where and in what types of habitat Africa's wonderful wildlife is most commonly found.

CHAPTER 5

THE BIG FIVE

The dangerous game is true African hunting.

Even as I write these lines I'm packing for a hunt in Ethiopia. If everything goes perfectly I will fire just one shot at a mountain nyala of the size I have long dreamed of. I cannot say that Africa's dangerous game is always the most important or even the most exciting. But I can say that the illustrious quintet that composes Africa's "Big Five"—elephant, rhino, buffalo, lion, and leopard—is what differentiates African hunting from that of all the other continents. There was a time when this was not so. Within living memory the Indian subcontinent and Southeast Asia held a greater variety of dangerous game than Africa: tiger, leopard, elephant, rhinoceros, several different wild oxen, and a couple of varieties of bear. Those days are over and are unlikely ever to return. The universe of hunting truly dangerous game has shrunk dramatically, leaving us the big bears of North America and Asia, the water buffalo and banteng of Australia's northern territories, and the African Big Five.

The difference between hunting dangerous game and all other hunting is quite simple. When hunting dangerous game, in an instant the tables can turn, and the hunter becomes the hunted. Any wild animal can be dangerous under certain circumstances, but with a grizzly bear, a leopard, or a buffalo, you know from the outset that there are risks involved, and this lends a special spice to the hunt that nothing else can replicate.

Though there is great potential for danger, actual charges are rare, and serious human injury or death even rarer. As a writer I have never sensationalized these unusual events, and as a hunter I surely do not seek them! To me there is enough spice in just knowing that the potential exists, and I do everything in my power to avoid allowing that potential to become a reality. You do this by only taking shots you are confident of, shooting straight, and using common sense. Before potential danger escalates into an attack, and before the attack results in injury (or worse) to someone in the party, the hunter has usually committed serious mistakes.

The most common mistake lies in wounding an animal. Very few charges result from an unwounded animal, although it is always possible that someone else, like a poacher, has committed the sin. If your first shot is in the right place with an adequate caliber and a good bullet, it's almost impossible to get into trouble.

Hunting Africa's dangerous game takes you into the real, unchanged Africa, where herds of buffalo and elephant roam and the lions still roar.

The second most common mistake lies in trusting too much in that first shot. The African adage is that "it's the dead ones that get up and kill you." This is not entirely correct. Properly stated, "it's the ones *you think* are dead that get up and kill you." When you approach any downed animal, especially a large and dangerous beast, common sense should tell you to approach from behind, where the animal can't see you, and to make absolutely certain the animal is dead before you close in. Charges make great film. You can create them if you work hard enough at it, but I view this as a fool's game. No matter who is behind the gun, not all charges can be stopped. They can come from quarters so close and angles so severe that, no matter how well you shoot, somebody is going to get run over. Doesn't sound like fun to me!

Even with serious mistakes, the worst remains a remote possibility. To some extent it depends on luck. I have done a great deal of buffalo hunting and have followed up several wounded buffalo, none of which ended in charges. I have had much less experience hunting lion and elephant, but I have seen two lion charges and have often dodged cow elephant. Many fine professional hunters, such as Harry Selby and Geoff Broom, have enjoyed extremely active careers without receiving so much as a scratch. However, in recent years several superb professional hunters of equal reputation (and probably equal talent and skill) have been hammered badly by wounded animals: Robin Hurt, Cotton Gordon, George Angelides. Sure, mistakes were made, usually by the client not shooting straight enough; but I have failed to shoot straight enough, and nobody has yet gotten hurt on my watch. My theory remains that luck is a factor, because not all charges can be stopped.

Like everything else in Africa, change is a constant, but here's a rundown on hunting the Big Five at the turn of the millennium, and my prediction on what the near future holds.

BUFFALO
(Syncerus caffer)

The buffalo is probably the most numerous of the Big Five, and certainly the most available to hunters. This is just fine with me, because I think a buffalo hunt is one of the most enjoyable experiences the African continent—and this hunter's world—has to offer. There are two things to remember when thinking about buffalo. First, there is more than one breed of buffalo in Africa. Second, buffalo do not occur (naturally or otherwise) in all areas.

The largest buffalo are the southern or Cape buffalo, ranging from South Africa north to Kenya and Uganda. Then the buffalo start to get smaller—first the Nile buffalo, centered in Sudan, then the northwestern buffalo of C.A.R. and points west. As they go west more individuals in a herd are red rather than black, clearly a transition. In the forests of Central and West Africa the buffalo are all red and very small and have separate horns that do not form a boss—the true dwarf buffalo. Northwestern buffalo are fairly common in northern C.A.R., Cameroon, and Burkina Faso. There are few opportunities to hunt Nile buffalo today; the only opportunity currently is in Ethiopia, where buffalo are hard to come by. The dwarf forest buffalo, one of the forest's great prizes, is very difficult to hunt. When most people think of African buffalo, they're thinking of the large Cape or southern variety.

Buffalo are herd animals, and where they exist there tends to be a lot of them . . . but they aren't everywhere. The South Africans are doing a wonderful job of reintroducing buffalo to their former range, but their propensity for carrying bovine disease is a serious problem. Limited availability of disease-free buffalo for reintroduction will continue to hinder this

We most often think of the large southern Cape buffalo, but there are several varieties of buffalo in Africa. This is a northwestern buffalo, much smaller in the body and horn and clearly a transition toward the red-colored dwarf forest buffalo.

Buffalo hunting is almost always a tracking hunt. Once you start a buffalo track you never know where it might lead you—but it's always exciting.

effort for many years to come. For this reason South Africa has good buffalo in the Kruger Park corridor, but you won't find them on the typical game ranch, nor will you find them in the ranch country in Zimbabwe or in most of Namibia. They need water, so you won't find them in arid areas, either.

Find relatively remote country with few cattle and permanent water and you will find buffalo. They are plentiful in Botswana's Chobe and Okavango regions; Zimbabwe's Zambezi Valley, and areas adjacent to Hwange and Gonarezhou Parks; and both the Kafue and Luangwa regions of Zambia. Mozambique's game was badly depleted during her long bush war, but there are pockets of good buffalo. Tanzania has vast numbers of buffalo in the Selous, western Tanzania, and the Rungwa. The high, cool hills of Masailand seem to grow big horns—but buffalo are not plentiful in Masailand and are becoming less so as the Masai cattle herds increase.

So where is the best place to hunt buffalo? I'm not sure it matters all that much. All of the areas that have southern buffalo have produced good buffalo, from South Africa to northern Tanzania. I tend to prefer areas that have lots of buffalo, because you usually have to sort your way through quite a few bulls to find a really good one. Many buffalo hunters take the first mature bull they get a crack at, and there's nothing wrong with that. Any fully mature bull with a hard boss, taken in fair chase by tracking and stalking, is a great trophy. However, the key to getting a really good buffalo is usually to take your time and look through as many herds as possible until you find what you're looking for. The first one you see might be the best one you'll ever see, but the more buffalo you have a chance to look at, the better your odds for finding a good one. Tanzania produces superb buffalo; so does Zimbabwe. The difference, I think, is that Zimbabwe's heavier thornbush makes it more difficult to find the big bulls. In other words, I don't believe Tanzania actually produces bigger buffalo than the southern areas, although the bigger buffalo may be somewhat easier to locate in more open areas like the Moyowosi and Masailand.

My own best buffalo came from Masailand, but I have taken very big buffalo in Zambia and Zimbabwe. I have also seen wonderful buffalo in Botswana's Okavango and in Tanzania's Selous Reserve. So long as the area has good numbers of buffalo, it doesn't matter so much where you hunt; it's far more important that you take your time.

I don't expect the buffalo situation to change much in years to come, except that, as the human population continues to expand, more land will be turned to agriculture and cattle. This is not good for buffalo; in the long term they will be relegated to parks and preserves and private conservancies. The hunting opportunities will become more limited and more costly, but there will be buffalo hunting in Africa for decades to come.

LEOPARD
(Panthera pardus pardus)

If the buffalo is the most numerous of the Big Five, the leopard is clearly the most widespread. The distinctive round pug marks of a leopard may be found along virtually any watercourse in sub-Saharan Africa, and in the suburbs of virtually any African city or town. It is impossible to count the nocturnal, secretive leopard, but estimates of its total population run into the millions. The collapse of the fur market, coupled with the leopard's increasing value as a trophy animal, has allowed the population to increase significantly in many areas, and this trend will continue.

Leopard has always been plentiful in the remote game areas of countries such as Tanzania, Zambia, Mozambique, and Botswana; and, despite a century of hunting, they have remained endemic in Zimbabwe's dense thornbush. Today, largely due to their value as a game animal, they are increasing rapidly in much of South Africa and Namibia. There are simply

It's often said that Zimbabwe doesn't have big buffalo, but the main reason is that it's often hard to sort through the herds in the thick bush. This Zambezi Valley bull, taken with Russ Broom, would be a keeper anywhere.

lots of places to hunt leopard, and in some cases a leopard safari is less costly than a hunt for Cape buffalo.

A leopard safari, however, is significantly different. A buffalo hunt of seven to ten days is usually successful; a leopard hunt is a time-consuming and very specialized endeavor. Even where there are lots of leopard, there are no guarantees. Leopard hunting is a game of strategy and patience. You hang baits where a leopard should find them. Once the baits are up you must check them daily and replenish them frequently. When the leopard strikes the bait, you build a blind and the waiting begins. Many hunters take a leopard their first night in a blind. I was not so lucky; over the course of several safaris I took a leopard on my sixty-fifth night in a blind.

Your chances are generally better in areas with lots of leopard, and your chances of getting a cat on bait increase if you hang all the baits where you can check on a daily basis. But all you need is one leopard to hit one bait and then return when you're waiting

A perfect setup as viewed from the blind. The leopard will be silhouetted against the sunset, taking advantage of the very last glimmer of daylight.

for him. It is best to seek out a really good cat hunter who thinks and speaks leopard, and then concentrate on leopard hunting. You can do some plains-game hunting as you check baits, but you must not get sidetracked by buffalo tracks or a search for a big kudu. The day you get pulled away to do something else is the day a big tom strikes the one bait you didn't check.

Even in a good area with a good hunter, you can hit a time when the cats simply aren't feeding on dead bait. It's more difficult when it's hot, and almost impossible late in the season after the warthogs and impala have dropped their young. And you can waste precious days waiting for a big cat that is too smart to return to a bait. If you concentrate on leopard hunting and your PH is a good cat hunter, you should expect about a 60 percent chance of success on a two-week hunt.

This suggests to me that a leopard hunt is a poor choice for a first African safari, where everything is new and exciting and you want to take a variety of antelope along the way. It would be better to save the leopard for a subsequent hunt when you can really concentrate. If you do that, I'm not certain it matters so much exactly where you hunt. Remote areas in Tanzania, Zambia, Mozambique, Central African Republic, Zimbabwe, and Botswana generally have leopard that are less sophisticated and easier to get on bait; leopard in the game ranch country of Zimbabwe, South Africa, and Namibia are often well educated and extremely nocturnal, somewhat reducing the chances for success. On the other hand, hunts in these areas are often less costly than in more remote areas, and your professional hunter's experience with leopard makes a huge difference no matter where you hunt. As time passes there will be fewer and fewer areas that hold "easy" leopard that jump into the bait tree in broad daylight, but leopard will continue to expand their range and multiply, and the hunting opportunities will only get better.

Leopard are becoming increasingly plentiful in most areas. Hunting them successfully is more a matter of how long, how hard, and how well you hunt, rather than where. John Sheehan, the author, and Russ Broom with a fine tom taken in Zimbabwe's Zambezi Valley.

A couple of outfitters in southern Africa are now using dogs to hunt leopard, with excellent success. This is not altogether new; it was commonly used for both leopard and lion a century ago and is very effective. Some sandy areas such as the Kalahari allow tracking, and a few lucky hunters will take leopard through a chance daylight encounter. But baiting remains the traditional and most common way to hunt leopard, and I doubt this will ever change.

LION
(Panthera leo leo)

The African lion is a prolific breeder, and so long as there is adequate prey the population will quickly build to large prides. Most parks in Africa hold good numbers of lion, so there need be no concern over the species' survival. In terms of lion hunting there are concerns. First, lion are fond of livestock, but ranchers and herdsmen aren't fond of lion. As more and more land turns to cattle and agriculture, the country where lion can roam and hunt continues to shrink. Second, it takes five to seven years for a male lion to reach maturity and grow the kind of mane that makes him a trophy. Even with the time to live and grow, not all male lion have the genetic propensity to grow good manes. Also, manes are generally poorer in hot areas with lots of thornbush. The bottom line is that there are now relatively few hunting areas in all of Africa that hold good numbers of well-maned lion. At this writing I would rate a really good lion with a luxurious mane the most difficult trophy among the Big Five, and perhaps the most difficult of all Africa's great prizes—and I expect lion hunting to become ever more limited and more difficult.

As is the case with the leopard, lion hunting is an extremely specialized and time-consuming sport. Essential elements are time and the willingness to concentrate on lion to the exclusion of all else. It is also extremely important to hunt in a really good area. Right now northern Botswana is

The author took this fine Zambian lion with Russ Broom quite a few years ago. Today a well-maned lion is one of the most difficult trophies in Africa, with few areas offering really good odds.

probably the best, due to an extremely limited quota, which has made lion hunting there extremely expensive. There are good areas in Zambia, especially in some of the Kafue blocks; and excellent areas in Tanzania, especially Rungwa and western Tanzania. Zimbabwe has some excellent lion hunting in the Hwange Park corridor and in some Zambezi Valley areas. The Kruger Park corridor holds good lion, meaning the Mozambique side as well as the South African side. "Sleeper" areas you don't hear much about are Central Africa's giant eland country and Ethiopia's Afar area.

Lion are often hunted adjacent to a national park, but it takes time and a bit of luck to catch a lion coming out of forbidden territory. In any case, it usually takes some time to get lion feeding on bait and to work a strategy to get a shot. Two weeks is minimal; three weeks, better still. Even so, there are very few areas today that offer odds as high as 50 percent for a well-maned lion. Chances are better for hunters willing

This is a good elephant for today, taken in Mozambique in 1989. We probably will never again see more than the very occasional hundred-pounder, but elephant hunting will get better and better over the next few years.

to take a large-bodied male without undue concern about length of mane, and there are more areas available to them.

ELEPHANT

(Loxodonta africana)

Elephant hunting, and Africa's elephant population, were probably at their nadir when the ban on ivory trade went into effect in 1989. At that time there were probably 700,000 wild elephant remaining in Africa—hardly an endangered population but definitely threatened in many areas. Today the elephant population has grown considerably, with most estimates ranging up to 1.1 million. Habitat loss is the elephant's greatest enemy, as it is for all African wildlife, but elephant numbers continue to increase. Many local populations are at or above optimum carrying capacity. Sport hunting of trophy bulls is not a viable means of controlling elephant populations, since the removal of a handful of older bulls does little to reduce the herd size. However, elephant hunting is and will continue to be viable because it generates revenue and provides local employment and meat.

These days elephant safaris and license fees are frighteningly high compared to what they used to be. We will never return to the days when multiple elephant licenses were part of a general-bag safari, but I do believe there will be more opportunity to hunt elephant over the next couple of decades than there is today. There probably will not be opportunity for really heavy ivory. Countries such as Zimbabwe, Botswana, Namibia, and South Africa have managed their elephant and have demonstrated a surplus. They will continue hunting, and they will produce the occasional 80-pounder and, once in a great while, a monster approaching (or exceeding) the hundred-pound mark. Unfortunately, none of these areas was historically known for heavy ivory, and you can't change genetics and history. The fact that some outfitters achieve average tusk weight of around sixty pounds is a genuine tribute to good hunting and good management; the elephant hunter in southern Africa who passes up a sixty-pounder must understand that he or she is bucking heavy odds to see anything bigger.

In my view there is greater potential for heavy ivory in Tanzania, where big tuskers were taken historically. Poaching greatly reduced Tanzania's elephants during the 1980s, but they are rebuilding, and the young bulls are growing ivory. The Selous Reserve is getting better every year, and while few of these small-bodied elephant will ever be hundred-pounders, in time seventy-pounders will again be relatively available. Cameroon is open but historically is not heavy ivory country. Adjacent C.A.R. was, and her elephant are making a comeback. I expect C.A.R. will someday reopen, and it could produce some very fine elephant, but never again the treasure trove of hundred-pounders that she was until the 1970s. Mozambique has very good elephant and when she reopens will be another area that will hold good numbers of seventy-pounders; but larger tusks will be very rare, as they always have been.

There are almost certainly pockets of big tuskers here and there in the thickest, remotest country, where even the indefatigable ivory poachers could not penetrate. The impenetrable Nile swamps of the Sudan, the forests of southwestern Ethiopia, and the great question mark of former Zaire all hold promise, but whether we will ever hunt these areas and be able to bring the ivory home is highly uncertain. My prediction is that elephant hunting is going to get better, and there will be more seventy-pounders and perhaps more eighty-pounders. But I do not believe tusks approaching the magical hundred-pound mark will ever again be a realistic goal.

RHINO
(Diceros bicornis and Ceratherium simum)

Some argue vehemently that the larger but more docile white rhino is not properly part of the Big Five; that the Big

White rhinos, once nearly extinct, have made a great comeback and are widely available to hunt today, but they are pricey! (Photo: Safari Press library)

Five ended when black rhino closed. I don't personally buy this, but to each his own. Certainly the recovery of the white rhino is one of the twentieth century's great conservation stories, while the destruction of the black rhino is one of its saddest chapters. Today white rhino hunting has stabilized, and I expect it to continue with justifiably high trophy fees for the relatively small number of trophy bulls. White rhino hunting is almost exclusively a South African show and has been since hunting resumed some twenty years ago, but there will be a little more rhino hunting in Namibia in years to come, and probably a few surplus bulls in Zimbabwe as well.

The real uncertainty surrounds the black rhino. The black rhino will never again be hunted in a free-range situation, but there are breeding populations in parks and reserves, both public and private, in South Africa and Zimbabwe. Protective measures have been extreme, but these animals are safe from poachers, and there are now surplus bulls past breeding age (and in the future there will be more). Unless the goal is to move the animals to safer areas, I am not in favor of the darting hunts for black rhino, but I am certainly in favor of hunting genuinely surplus animals, and the astronomical trophy fees can provide a genuine boost to recovery efforts. I believe we will see very little of this kind of black rhino hunting in years to come. Regrettably, it will be similar to today's white rhino hunting—a pale shadow of the rhino hunting that ended when Tanzania and Zambia closed the last open-range black rhino hunting in the early 1980s.

Which is the most dangerous of the Big Five? It's an old question, and African hunters far more experienced than I have answered it many times and in many ways. But this discussion wouldn't be complete without my opinion. *All* of the Big Five can be extremely dangerous, including the white rhino. Unwounded and unmolested, I think cow elephant are probably the most dangerous, but few sport hunters actively pursue elephant cows, and a charge from a bull elephant is much less likely.

In the event of a charge, the leopard is the most likely to get through the guns and get its teeth and claws into you. This is because of its camouflage in shadowed bush, the close cover it generally chooses when it lies in wait, and its size and the incredible speed of its attack. This opinion is borne out by the substantial number of professional hunters and trackers—and the occasional client—that are bitten and clawed by leopard annually. The damage is often severe, and the experience must be horrible (Lord knows I don't want to go through it). Thanks to modern antibiotics, most people survive a leopard mauling and recover more or less completely.

In the past few years buffalo have killed several people, both PHs and clients, and many more have been horribly injured. Permanent disability at some level is almost certain if a buffalo gets through to you, and many old hands rate the buffalo as the

The author took this heavy-horned white rhino on the Palala River in South Africa with Willem van Dyk. It was a great hunt, but all rhino hunting now is a shadow of what it used to be, and probably will not recover.

most dangerous. I think the recent rash of incidents is caused by two factors, often in concert. With habitat shrinking, buffalo are hunted today in thicker cover than ever before. There is a big difference between hunting buffalo in savanna woodland and hunting it in the thick *jess*. The other factor is that we are losing the generations of professional hunters who grew up shooting leopards out of the chicken coop and buffalo out of the cow pasture, and who underwent years of rigorous apprenticeship before going solo. Many younger professional hunters are good lads, keen and eager, but with limited exposure to hunting dangerous game. Some accidents are directly attributable to lack of experience, while others happened because, as I said earlier, not all charges can be stopped.

Buffalo can be very dangerous, but I do not rate them at the top. In my book, that honor goes to lion. I respect them all, and my palms sweat whenever I'm close to them. The buffalo is huge and hard to stop, but whether you can stop it or not depends largely on the ground where it chooses to make its stand. You can see it, you can hit it, and you can stop it if there is time. Elephant are much the same, except that a non-fatal hit may turn an elephant. When the lion comes, it comes low and fast, a difficult target that you may or may not have a shot at before it's too late . . . and unless you have a double-barrel, you will probably have just one shot. The leopard is even faster and more difficult to hit well on the charge, but a leopard often leaps from hunter to tracker to client, savaging each, then melting back into the brush. The lion usually picks just one target and is unlikely to be turned. If you can't stop the lion, it will finish the job if it can. I respect them all, but the lion I fear.

CHAPTER 6

THE SPIRAL HORNS

The beautiful and challenging spiral-horned antelope represent some of Africa's greatest prizes.

Africa is blessed with the greatest variety of wildlife on earth, and much of this diversity is found in her antelope. Counting all the races and subspecies, there are easily more than a hundred types of antelope—and then there are the pigs, zebras, cats, thick-skinned game, and all the rest! Of course this great cornucopia doesn't all occur in one region, and nobody will ever hunt all the African game. Most of us plan our safaris with a few key trophies in mind.

It is not up to me to suggest what African trophies should be most important to you. We develop our own preferences based on eye appeal, challenge, style of hunting, and habitat. I think dangerous game most typifies African hunting, and for me the spiral-horned antelope follow closely. Many would reverse this order, and I wouldn't argue. Come to think of it, I have spent far more time and money in the pursuit of the spiral-horned antelope than in hunting the Big Five!

Part of the reason is that there are nine principal varieties of spiral-horned antelope, and several have multiple subspecies. Some of these antelope are widespread and relatively common; others are restricted in range and require very specialized safaris to the far-flung corners of the continent. All possess the characteristics that lead to a wonderful hunting experience: beauty, grace, and challenge. All are cunning, wary, cover-dwelling antelope, and the outcome of the hunt is never certain.

I'm sure that I will never tire of tracking buffalo, but I will also never tire of hunting the spiral horns. The most common of the group, bushbuck and kudu, are among my favorite hunts, but I have hunted them all multiple times, and the lure of the entire tribe never diminishes.

I am writing these lines in the shade of some tall heather, high up in Ethiopia's Bale Mountains. My buddy, Joe Bishop, is taking a nap off to my right. Three days ago I realized a longstanding dream by taking a wonderful mountain nyala. Joe is still struggling for his, and I'm having just as much fun struggling along with him. I'm wondering if I still have enough time—and whether I can make enough money—to hunt this and all the other spiral horns just once more!

The grouping of nine spiral horns is not a strictly scientific classification. It is a loose "hunter's grouping" based on horn similarities: They all have smooth horns that twist or spiral upward around a keel. Two distinct genera are represented. In genus *Tragelaphus*, the "true" spiral horns, you find greater kudu, lesser kudu, bushbuck, sitatunga, nyala, bongo, and mountain nyala. Common eland and giant or Lord Derby eland are of genus *Taurotragus*. I doubt that any hunter, past or present, has ever taken all of the races and subspecies, and in today's Africa no one ever will. The nine principals are huntable today, which has not always been so. Greater kudu, bushbuck, sitatunga, and common eland also have multiple subspecies (and record-book categories) that are huntable, but not all subspecies can now be hunted, and some probably never will be again. It is unlikely that western giant eland or Kenya bongo will ever again be hunted. Current politics also place Nile bushbuck and Sesse Islands sitatunga beyond our reach.

Most of us with "spiral-horn fever" content ourselves with the nine principal varieties, although over the course of several safaris a few of the subspecies will naturally come along. For those who get the fever really bad, a lifetime pursuit awaits! I will not attempt to discuss all of the races and subspecies, but the following is my spin on spiral-horn hunting today, from the least to the most difficult.

NYALA
(Tragelaphus angasi)

The beautiful nyala is one of the most restricted in range, confined naturally to Mozambique, Malawi, the Zululand region of South Africa, and just a corner of Zimbabwe. There have

A very good southern greater kudu taken in Botswana. At this time of year the kudu were concentrated along the sand rivers; the author saw more than fifty kudu bulls before taking this beautiful bull.

been times when this exquisite antelope was among the more difficult prizes. Today I rate it the easiest because the bulk of the population and hunting is concentrated in well-managed game ranches in South Africa. Like all the spiral horns, nyala prefer heavy cover, so where they are scarce—as in most areas of Zimbabwe and modern Mozambique—they are very difficult to hunt. Game ranching, by the way, has also extended the nyala's range to all regions of South Africa and also to Zimbabwe and a few spots in Namibia. A few days' effort, glassing, and still-hunting in good country will usually produce success and is well worthwhile. With a long, chocolate-brown coat, orange underparts, white highlights, and beautiful lyre-shaped horns, the nyala is one of the most striking of all African antelope.

GREATER KUDU
(Tragelaphus strepsiceros)

With its gray, white-striped body and spectacular corkscrew-shaped horns, the greater kudu is probably the most recognizable of all African antelope and certainly the most prized among hunters. Its spectacular appearance rates this attention, but its popularity is partly due to the wealth of great literature spawned by kudu hunting. From Roosevelt to Maydon and Hemingway to Ruark, vintage Africana describes hunting the "gray ghost" as a difficult, all-consuming pursuit with limited chance for success. Kudu are shy and wary, spending most of their time in thick thornbush, but, historically, they were hunted in the wrong place, and this contributed to the legend of their difficulty to hunt.

In East Africa (which now means Tanzania), greater kudu have always been scarce and hard to come by. In Ethiopia the Abyssinian subspecies is often more difficult to hunt than mountain nyala. In Chad and C.A.R., the small western greater kudu may well be the ultimate spiral horn. But in South

Africa, Namibia, and Zimbabwe, the greater kudu is the most common large antelope in most areas, and it is plentiful in parts of Mozambique, Botswana, and Zambia as well. In all of these areas a greater kudu is part of a normal bag on a seven- to ten-day safari, which speaks much for its availability. And thanks to excellent game management in southern Africa, trophy quality just keeps getting better.

Regardless of how plentiful, the greater kudu is a wonderful creature, challenging and fun to hunt. It deserves its top position on most first-timers' wish lists, and it is still near the top of mine!

BUSHBUCK
(Tragelaphus scriptus)

The bushbuck is by far the most widespread of all the spiral horns, existing in dozens of races from the southern edge of

Professional hunter Rudy Lubin with a good harnessed bushbuck from the C.A.R. The various races of bushbuck vary more in appearance than do other spiral horns, with the harnessed bushbuck the most colorful.

the Sahara to South Africa's Cape. The record books have distilled these confusing and disputable subspecies into eight categories, mostly reflecting regional groupings.

Hunting the bushbuck varies little across its range, though local densities vary. It is the smallest spiral horn, a classy little antelope that prefers dense riverine thickets and thornbush hillsides. It is rarely taken by accident and usually requires careful still-hunting in good habitat in the early morning and late evening. Present in most African hunting areas, the bushbuck is often overlooked in pursuit of more glamorous prizes. This is unfortunate, because seriously hunting bushbuck is one of Africa's greatest delights. Provided one is willing to invest a few mornings or evenings to the pursuit, most hunting areas will produce bushbuck. These days the best opportunities for really good trophies are probably southern Zimbabwe and northern South Africa, where Limpopo bushbuck seem to be getting bigger and bigger.

COMMON ELAND

(Taurotragus oryx)

There is nothing common about the common eland! It is a giant of an antelope, weighing as much as a ton—more than any buffalo. Both bulls and cows grow horns that twist about a prominent keel, but the horns of a bull are wonderfully thick and impressive. Despite its size, the eland is as agile as a gazelle, and, if spooked, it will eat up many miles in a seemingly effortless swinging, ground-eating trot. The eland is also one of the most consistently wary of all antelope.

Found in several races from southern Ethiopia to the Cape of South Africa, it is plentiful enough that it is often taken incidental to other hunting. A chance encounter with a big eland bull is a great opportunity but misses the really fine experience of specifically hunting eland. This usually involves tracking until you spot a herd, then very slow and ticklish stalking while you try to distinguish the thick horns of a bull from the long, thin cow horns. Eland are primarily browsers that will roam many miles in search of favored food sources. There are many good places to hunt them, but I would choose private land in Zimbabwe, Zambia's Kafue region, and Tanzania's Selous Reserve. By the way, eland venison is the very finest wild meat in all the world!

LESSER KUDU
(*Tragelaphus imberbis*)

In the old days of East Africa the lesser kudu was considered common game, but no longer. With Kenya,

It isn't all that difficult to tell the difference between eland bulls and cows. Not only are bull horns much thicker, but cows lack the dark, woolly skullcap on the forehead. This is a huge East African eland from Luke Samaras's Selous Game Reserve concession.

The author took this wonderful lesser kudu in Masailand with Michel Mantheakis. Today the only two places where lesser kudu can still be hunted are northern Tanzania and Ethiopia, making this once-common animal a fairly difficult prize.

One of the difficulties with lesser kudu is that they tend to be thinly distributed in dry thornbush country, and it's hard to know where to look. Joe Bishop and Ethiopian outfitter Colonel Negussie Eshete glass typical lesser kudu country in the Danakil.

Somalia, Uganda, and Sudan closed, the only remaining opportunities are northeastern Tanzania and Ethiopia. Both regions do offer a wonderful variety of game, so the lesser kudu is rarely the sole object of a safari—but the lesser kudu usually requires a lot of looking. It is a creature of arid thornbush, rarely concentrated and too light-footed to track in the hard-baked country it calls home. It is usually hunted by glassing or moving slowly, by vehicle or on foot, through good country. The lesser kudu is not uncommon where it occurs, but nowhere today is success certain. I believe the horn average, and very possibly the hunter success, is a bit higher in Ethiopia than in Masailand, but the real secret to bagging lesser kudu is to spend plenty of time hunting them. It can be difficult to find the time, because a safari in lesser kudu country is likely to be built around equally time-consuming pursuits such as cat hunting.

All hunts for multiple species come down to priorities, but the lesser kudu is well worth the time and effort required. In appearance it is about half the size of a greater kudu, very dainty and elegant with miniature kudu horns and comparatively larger ears. I can never decide which of the spiral horns I like the best, but I would never overlook the lesser kudu.

SITATUNGA
(Tragelaphus spekei)

The swamp-dwelling sitatunga is one of the spiral horns that requires an extremely specialized safari. It lives primarily in and around papyrus reed beds along lakes and rivers from Angola to the Nile and westward through the bulge of West Africa. As with the bushbuck, sitatunga comprise several record-book categories based primarily on regional groupings; scientists have never fully agreed on the various subspecies.

The bongo is one of the most dramatic of all the world's big game. It is not only colorful but represents some of the world's most difficult hunting.

Unlike the races of bushbuck, which often differ dramatically in color and size, there is relatively little visual difference among the races of sitatunga.

The difficulty of hunting them depends, like everything else, on the local population density and the hunter's ability to penetrate their habitat. This last is the key with sitatunga; in all cases you must penetrate their swampy environment to hunt them. However, the country surrounding most sitatunga haunts holds a variety of other game. So the hunter has to choose between a relatively short but highly specialized safari and a week or so of swamp hunting set aside on a safari that includes a variety of other game.

The sitatunga is a strange-looking antelope, with an unkempt, mousy-brown hide, a short, rodentlike face, and, of course, the nose chevron of the Tragelaphus clan. Its hoofs are elongated, an adaptation to its watery environment, and its lovely horns form a loose spiral, rarely completing a second turn. The sitatunga is always difficult

Typical sitatunga haunts at dawn. Glassing papyrus reed beds from a raised platform, or machan, is the most common way to hunt sitatunga—and it's glorious to watch the swamps come alive.

to hunt but is actually quite plentiful in many areas, especially Botswana's Okavango and Zambia's Bangweulu region. In some areas you can pole silently along in a dugout and surprise feeding sitatunga, but the most prevalent technique is glassing likely areas from machans. Provided you allow plenty of time and avoid the full moon (when sitatunga become nocturnal), hunting for the "swamp fairy" is quite successful—but rarely easy.

LORD DERBY ELAND

(Taurotragus derbianus)

Everything I've said about common eland applies to Lord Derby or giant eland. I am not certain giant eland are bigger in the body than common eland—certainly not substantially so—but the horns are much longer and more impressive. Derby eland are also more colorful, with a striking black collar and black-and-white stockings. The Derby eland is, to me, the most

The various races of sitatunga are similar in appearance, but the Zambezi variety is the most plentiful and probably grows the longest horns. This is a superb bull from Zambia's Bangweulu, taken with Russ Broom.

impressive African trophy. I do not think it is naturally warier than the common eland, but it lives in more difficult country—the vast, roadless Terminalia forest of northern C.A.R. and Cameroon. It is hunted almost invariably by tracking—and you will follow the tracks many miles in extreme heat.

In C.A.R., success is very high on two-week giant eland hunts, so I do not rate the Derby eland as difficult as the bongo. It is a far more physically challenging hunt, however—and this animal is worth every drop of sweat.

BONGO

(Tragelaphus euryceros)

Burnt orange in color, with prominent white side-stripes, black-and-white facial highlights, and thick, smooth, gently

Joe Bishop, the author, and Colonel Negussie Eshete with Bishop's big mountain nyala, described by the Ethiopians as "a mountain nyala of before." Taken in March 2000, this was the largest one taken in nearly fifteen years. Larger bulls have been taken since Joe's bull, so there is hope for the mountain nyala.

spiraling horns, the bongo is one of the world's most fantastic creatures. If it lived in herds on the open plains it would still be a dramatic trophy. Instead, it lives in the thick forest, offering some of the world's most difficult and challenging hunting. While I consider bongo more difficult to bag than Derby eland, I find the hunting physically easier, simply because it never gets really hot in the shaded forest. Others might disagree.

The western bongo occupies a broad range across the forest belt from southern Sudan to West Africa and south through the Congo forests. Today it is hunted in C.A.R., Cameroon, and Congo. Although never easy, western bongo is surprisingly common in some parts of the great forest. In the old days, bongo hunting was pure tracking in the virgin forest, an exceptionally difficult pursuit. Logging has opened up roads and increased access; this, combined with the use of dogs, has greatly improved success in modern bongo hunting. Even so, the African forest offers some of the most difficult hunting on earth. Visibility is measured in feet, there is little wildlife to be seen (often for days on end), and the hunter must constantly stoop and crawl to negotiate the latticework of vines and branches. There are no easy options for bongo hunting except to hunt bongo. Depending on your luck, it can take a long time!

MOUNTAIN NYALA
(Tragelaphus buxtoni)

Found only in Ethiopia's high country southeast of Addis Ababa, the mountain nyala is the most restricted in range, has probably the smallest population, and offers the most limited hunting opportunity of all the spiral horns. Relatively few sportsmen have pursued it. Despite its scarcity, it is one of the great legends of the hunting world. So I continue to be amazed at how few hunters have heard of this animal and how many think it is just an offshoot of the South African nyala.

The mountain nyala is the size of the greater kudu but is more heavily built. It is brown with muted white side-stripes, white spots on its flanks, and a prominent white nose chevron. Its horns, although larger than those of the southern nyala, do often replicate the lyre shape of the southern nyala's horns, hence its name. Its local name, translated, means "highland kudu," which is more appropriate. Ivor Buxton, who discovered it in 1908, originally called it a "mountain bushbuck," which is actually the most appropriate. Fellow spiral-horn nut Chris Kinsey recently took samples for DNA testing, and the results indicate that the mountain nyala is genetically closer to the bushbuck than to the greater kudu and is quite distant from the nyala.

The mountain nyala generally lives in the high heather, usually above ten thousand feet elevation, where the animal is hard to find, hard to see, and hard to shoot. Habitat loss and local meat poaching are its greatest enemies, and until recently both hunter success and trophy quality were dwindling rapidly. In 1999 my old friend Colonel Negussie opened a new area near Bale National Park, and since then has achieved success on good bulls that is unprecedented in the last twenty years. Obviously this is good news, but the bad news is that opportunity is very limited. The combined quota for mountain nyala among all of Ethiopia's few outfitters is less than a dozen bulls. But with quotas, size restrictions, and genuine conservation efforts, there is hope for the mountain nyala, my pick for Africa's greatest trophy.

The bushbuck is by far the most widespread of all African spiral-horn antelope; however, they are often far from easy to hunt. (Photo: Safari Press library)

Oh, yes, I wouldn't want to leave you hanging. I'm still on a mountain in Ethiopia, but early this morning Joe Bishop took a huge mountain nyala, the biggest in years. The Ethiopians described it as "a nyala of before." It is one of the most wonderful creatures I've ever seen. Perhaps in the future more bulls will grow to this size.

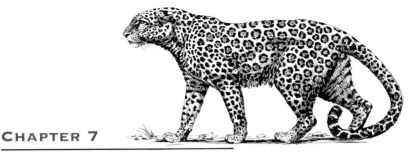

CHAPTER 7

THE GLAMOROUS GAME

In the previous chapter we dwelled upon Africa's nine spiral-horned antelopes. This group is certainly the most recognizable and possibly the most sought-after of Africa's nondangerous game—but the nine spiral horns are just the tip of the iceberg. It would be not only presumptuous but downright wrong to attempt to suggest what animals should appeal the most to you and what trophies you should plan your safaris around. These decisions are up to you and should be based entirely upon your own hunting interests, not what anyone else says you should pursue. While the Big Five is a well-established class, as are the spiral-horned antelope, the next few chapters become very subjective.

In this chapter I will discuss several African animals that I consider especially beautiful, impressive, and challenging—or some combination of the three. These are animals that I might place near the top, or at the very top, of my wish list on a safari to the areas where these animals occur. In Chapter 8 I'll discuss some of the animals that I consider "common game," the spice that holds a safari together but is almost never a primary goal. Chapter 9 will then conclude with a discussion of the pygmy antelopes. Some of you might wish to switch some of these around, and that's perfectly OK with me. For instance, I find the smaller antelope very interesting, but not so interesting that I would plan a safari around them. Many hunters do. Now that we've covered the Big Five and the spiral horns, I will cover some of the other animals that I also consider great prizes: sable antelope; roan; oryx;

waterbuck, lechwe, and kob; aoudad and ibex; giant forest hog; and vaal rhebok. Again, my priorities don't have to be yours. You may attach greater significance to some of the reedbuck or species of antelope in the genus Damaliscus, especially local rarities like the bontebok or Senegal hartebeest; or to some of the forest duikers or tough little prizes like suni and grysbok. This is fine with me, but it will take a little time to work our way through Africa's wonderful plethora of game, so you'll have to be patient!

SABLE ANTELOPE
(Hippotragus niger)

When Cornwallis Harris "discovered" this wonderful animal back in the 1830s, he described it as the most wonderful animal known to man. He was not wrong. With a striking black coat, white underparts, and white facial highlights, the

Sable antelope are a creature of the mopane and miombo woodlands, but they don't stay in the thickest cover and are quite visible. Females and youngsters are more brownish; only the males are jet-black, and they stand out—but not in heavy shadow.

sable is just plain gorgeous. With its powerful shoulders and erect black mane, it is impressive. And with its long, sharp, scimitar-shaped horns, it is awesome. The sable antelope is probably Africa's most beautiful antelope. The only reason it doesn't rank alongside great prizes such as bongo and mountain nyala is the simple fact that it is relatively easy to hunt.

Mind you, Africa is a big place, and any animal that is locally uncommon can be darned hard to find. But the sable is a herd animal that prefers relatively open woodland. Being relatively visible, the sable is not extremely difficult to locate and stalk in country where it is plentiful. Unlike many species, both males and females grow similar horns. This can be difficult for beginners, and indeed I made a horrible mistake the first time I hunted sable—but there is really no excuse. While sable cows occasionally grow horns that are impressive in length, the circumference of bull horns is much greater. Much more important, sable cows are

A nice sable from western Tanzania, taken on the Ugalla River with Geoff Broom.

brownish in body color, as are young bulls. Only fully mature bulls have the glossy, jet-black color, and they stand out readily.

Three races have been identified: the common sable of southern Africa; the East African or Roosevelt sable of coastal Kenya; and the giant sable of central Angola. The fabulous giant sable, with horns exceeding sixty inches, was feared to have become extinct during Angola's long civil war. Apparently a few survive, which is wonderful news—but I doubt giant sable will ever again be hunted. Recent studies suggest that some of Tanzania's northernmost sable may actually be of the Roosevelt race, so some of us may have hunted this sable unknowingly. But for now, the sable we hunt is the common sable, found discontinuously from northern South Africa through Botswana, Zimbabwe, and Zambia to the southern fringes of Tanzania's Masailand.

Sable are sensitive to drought and do not adapt well to human intrusion. Also, it takes a long time for sable bulls to mature, and the demand for sable antelope has long since outstripped the supply. The result is that there are now relatively few areas that have numbers of good sable. Quotas tend to be low, and modern sable hunters can expect to pay increasingly high trophy fees and escalating "minimum days" to have a chance for this animal. The best areas today, in terms of both numbers and trophy quality, are concessions around Zambia's Kafue National Park, Tanzania's Rungwa area, and Zimbabwe's Matetsi; but sable bulls with horns measuring more than forty-three inches are common nowhere today.

ROAN ANTELOPE
(Hippotragus equinus)

Although much larger in body than the sable, the roan antelope is a close relative, with similar build and horns that follow an identical curve but are much shorter. Rufous in color and with much larger ears, the roan is a beautiful and imposing antelope, although not so attractive as its coal-black cousin.

The roan of Zambia are considered Angolan roan, one of several races. Average horn length varies somewhat, but the various subspecies differ little in appearance.

A very good gemsbok bull taken with Dirk de Bod in the Kalahari Desert in Namibia. The gemsbok is the most plentiful and most easily obtained of the three huntable oryx—but bulls of this quality are hard to find.

The roan is much more widespread, occurring discontinuously in several races from South Africa north to Sudan and all the way across the continent to West Africa. It is not found in the forest, the deserts, or the mountains. The roan is a creature of open woodlands, whether mopane, *miombo*, or Terminalia, preferring more open country than the sable. Historically, roan antelope were fairly common, but their less-impressive horns rendered them much less desirable than the more localized sable. In modern Africa, it appears that the roan is less tolerant of human incursion into its domain than many other species. Over time, it has become less and less common across much of its range, and opportunities to hunt the roan have shrunk dramatically. The result is that a good roan antelope is now considered by many a superior trophy to a sable, although not nearly so impressive.

Roan tend to occur in small herds, and one frequently encounters solitary bulls. Although many references list roan as the second-largest antelope after eland, I'm not at all convinced that roan outweigh kudu, bongo, or mountain nyala. However, they are much larger than sable and certainly big enough to allow tracking if soil conditions are right, which they usually are not. The semi-open woodlands that roan prefer are not always conducive to glassing, though they generally offer some visibility. So the only way to really hunt roan is simply to spend a lot of time in the right country until you encounter the right species of antelope. Obviously, this is a hit-or-miss situation, but many African antelope are like that.

Roan are generally regarded as one of the few "fierce" antelope; their horns are short but wicked, and roan know how to use them. When I took my first one, in Zambia back in 1983, my professional hunter, Bill Illingsworth, quickly exhorted me, "Stay away from that thing!" Although sable, oryx, and bongo can also be dangerous when wounded, of all the antelope only roan and bushbuck have a reputation for truculence.

There are several subspecies of roan that appear in five different record-book categories. The races do get a bit smaller in the horn as you move from north to south, but beyond that they are virtually indistinguishable. The species has long been protected in Botswana and Zimbabwe, but it is available on a few game ranches in South Africa and Namibia. Roan remains huntable in Zambia, Tanzania, C.A.R., and Cameroon, and is the primary prize in West African countries such as Burkina Faso, Togo, and Senegal. Roan are where you find them and, like sable, are generally not that difficult to approach if you can find them. The best places to hunt roan are probably Tanzania's Rungwa and northern Cameroon. In both C.A.R. and Cameroon the large western roan shares the savanna woodland with Derby eland, but in C.A.R. it is my impression that Derby eland are far more plentiful than roan. Moving west into C.A.R., roan are more plentiful than eland, according to most reports.

ORYX

(Oryx gazella)

There are three distinct subspecies of O. gazella: the gemsbok or giant oryx of southern Africa; the fringe-eared oryx of northern Tanzania and southern Kenya; and the beisa oryx, ranging from northern Kenya up through the horn of Africa. The other two great desert antelope of the Sahara, the scimitar-horned oryx and the addax, would surely be listed among Africa's great prizes if this were being written twenty years ago. Regrettably, poaching—much by soldiers with automatic weapons—has virtually exterminated these wonderful creatures. Their very survival in their native range is in question, and there is almost no chance that they will ever again return to huntable numbers in their native range. So, while we mustn't forget the wonderful Sahara safaris of the past, in modern hunting literature it is appropriate to speak of only three varieties of oryx. There is also an Angolan subspecies of gemsbok that may someday be huntable again.

The three oryx are actually quite similar, gray in the body with black and white on the underparts and legs and a dramatic black-and-white face mask. All have straight, sharp horns that are heavily ringed about halfway up, and both sexes have similar horns. Cow horns are often longer than bull horns but are always thinner. Body size among the three types is also very similar; despite its nickname of "giant oryx," the gemsbok is not substantially larger than the northern oryx. The fringe-eared oryx definitely has the shortest horns of the three, and its white-and-black markings are generally the most muted. However, the most distinctive characteristic is the black tufts at the ear tips. Today the fringe-eared oryx is hunted only in Tanzania's

The black lechwe is the shortest-horned of the lechwe. Few of them are actually black, so the visual difference between black, Kafue, and red lechwe isn't always dramatic. Robert E. Petersen took this one with Austin Wienand.

Masailand. The beisa oryx, now hunted only in Ethiopia, has substantially longer horns and somewhat more brilliant markings. Most brilliantly marked of all is the gemsbok, also differentiated by larger, more rounded ears and substantially longer horns. In terms of horn length, the gemsbok really is a giant oryx. Most of Botswana's Kalahari is now closed, but gemsbok are readily hunted throughout most of South Africa and Namibia, making them the most readily accessible of the three oryx.

The oryx is a dry land antelope, ranging from dry thornbush to semi-desert to true desert. In the desert environment it may go for long periods without drinking, taking moisture from dew and desert melons. Because of their open habitat, oryx can be glassed from great distances, so in good country finding them is not the big problem. Stalking close enough for a shot, and then picking the best bull from all those straight horns, are the two primary challenges of oryx

The Barbary sheep, or aoudad, is easily one of Africa's greatest prizes, and also offers one of Africa's most unusual hunts. This one was taken by the author with Alain Lefol in Chad in January 2001.

115

hunting. The fringe-eared oryx remains part of a normal bag in Tanzania's Masailand concessions, and beisa oryx are still plentiful in both the Danakil and Omo Valley in Ethiopia. The best gemsbok tend to come from desert areas, with the Namib and Kalahari of Namibia producing the best trophies currently available.

WATERBUCK, LECHWE, AND KOB
(Kobus ellipsiprymnus, K. lechwe, and K. kob)

This is a large and varied group. None of these species is particularly hard to hunt where they occur, but virtually all (except the widespread waterbuck) are extremely localized. All are very attractive antelopes that tend to prefer flood plain or riverine habitat. The stately waterbuck, though hardly

The various races of lechwe are localized antelope found in marshy areas and flood plains. These are black lechwe, found only near Zambia's Lake Bangweulu. Lechwe are generally so numerous that they offer little challenge—but they are local rarities, and you have to be where they are in order to hunt them.

rare and rarely elusive, is one of Africa's most regal antelope. All of the lechwe are magnificent, and all are likely to be found on the open flood plains in herds of thousands. However, you must go to Zambia's Bangweulu to hunt black lechwe, to the Kafue Flats for Kafue lechwe, and to Botswana or western Zambia for red lechwe. And right now you may not hunt the most beautiful lechwe of all, the Nile lechwe, because Sudan is closed. The closure is due to a long civil war, so the current status of this important animal is very much in question.

The kobs could perhaps be described as lechwe with short, thick horns. Neither the Uganda kob nor the white-eared kob is huntable today, but the western kob is found across a broad stretch of sub-Saharan Africa from C.A.R. westward. Far to the south, in Zambia and southwestern Tanzania, the puku (*Kobus vardoni*) is actually a close relative of the kobs, and was once called Vardon's kob.

Any animal that is locally scarce can be darned difficult to hunt, but under normal conditions none of these animals are particularly difficult to locate or especially challenging to hunt. However, the kobs and lechwes are all beautiful creatures, and their presence (or absence) in a trophy collection instantly defines where a hunter has been (or has not been).

The waterbuck is hardly localized, but exists in many races literally from top to bottom. It is properly "common game," except that it is such a dramatic and beautiful trophy that I cannot describe it as such. The common waterbuck has an elliptical rump ring, while the defassa waterbuck does not. Both have several subspecies that can be classified in several record-book categories—but I defy anyone to classify waterbuck based on mounted heads! There are regional differences and trends, but rarely are they definitive. The waterbuck has an oily coat with a distinctive odor, and the

A western kob, taken by the author with Rudy Lubin along the Chinko River in eastern C.A.R. The western kob is the most widespread of the several kobs, and the only one currently huntable.

legend is that the meat is inedible. This is simply not true; as table fare waterbuck aren't fabulous, but secretions from their skin glands have no impact on the meat.

The longest-horned waterbuck tend to come from South Africa and Zimbabwe, but there are also very good sing-sing waterbuck in C.A.R. and Cameroon, and Ethiopia's Danakil produces superb East African defassa waterbuck. The shortest-horned waterbuck is the Crawshay defassa waterbuck of Zambia's Kafue region. Regardless of race, with its stately carriage, luxurious coat, and thick, gently curving horns, a good waterbuck is a fine trophy. Few hunts plan safaris with a waterbuck as a primary objective, but you should not pass up a chance to take a good bull of any race.

AOUDAD AND IBEX
(Ammotragus lervia and Capra ibex nubiana)

The Barbary sheep (aoudad) and the Nubian ibex, although only vaguely related, are considered together for two reasons. First, these two are the last of North Africa's great desert game, now that scimitar-horned oryx and addax are virtually gone. Second, while Barbary sheep and Nubian ibex do not occur in the same area, each requires a specialized safari, and serious African hunters highly prize them both.

The Nubian ibex is actually one of two African ibex. The walia ibex of Ethiopia's Simen Mountains is a much larger, thicker-horned animal. Although its numbers are low, it appears that the walia ibex's slide toward extinction has been halted. The walia has been protected for many years, and it is unlikely that it will be hunted. The Nubian ibex actually has a large range, occupying the Red Sea Hills from Eritrea up through Sudan, Egypt, the Sinai, and on into Israel. There has been much uncontrolled meat hunting through most of its range, and the only hunting currently available is in the

Red Sea Hills of Sudan. Despite a current moratorium on hunting in Egypt, reports of poaching continue—but the range of the ibex is very large in this country. In Israel (which is not Africa) the Nubian ibex has been well protected, so there is potential for greater opportunity on either side of the Red Sea.

The aoudad once occupied a very large range in most desert mountains from northwestern Sudan to Morocco. Like all North African game, the population has been badly depleted by decades of civil war and uncontrolled poaching. A reintroduced population in Morocco is doing well. About a decade ago there seemed a strong possibility that Morocco might open limited sport hunting, but this never happened and seems unlikely now. A few aoudad were taken recently in

The extent to which an animal is prized depends on beauty, difficulty to hunt, and availability. The little dorcas gazelle inhabits the fringes of the Sahara, and until Chad reopened in the late '90s was almost impossible to hunt.

Sudan, but numbers are low. So until very recently it appeared that native-range hunting for Barbary sheep was almost a thing of the past. The reopening of Chad has changed this. The Ennedi Plateau still holds good numbers of this wonderful animal, and the hunting is excellent. This classic hunt in North Africa's desert mountains is a sheep hunt unlike any other African hunting, and it is now an available and extremely successful hunting experience.

GIANT FOREST HOG
(Hylochoerus meinertzhageni)

Discovered by Colonel Richard Meinertzhagen early in the twentieth century, the secretive and strange-looking giant

A good giant forest hog, taken by the author with Jacques Lemaux in C.A.R. The author didn't get a bongo that trip, but the forest hog was an acceptable consolation prize—they're actually less common and far more difficult to hunt than bongo!

forest hog was one of the last large mammals on earth to be identified. It is not larger than a really big European wild boar, but it is a very large and imposing creature that, in appearance, is like a cross between a warthog and a wild boar. The giant forest hog actually occupies a very large range— not only the forests of Central and West Africa but also Mount Kenya and the Aberdares, the forests and high country of Ethiopia, and southern Sudan. The problem is that this game is common in few areas and is extremely nomadic, meaning hunters find it almost impossible to predict just where they might encounter the animal in its thick habitat. Usually it is taken incidental to bongo hunting, but the giant forest hog is far less common than bongo. This fact, coupled with the extreme difficulty in specifically hunting giant forest hog, places it among Africa's great prizes. The best opportunity to hunt it is probably in Ethiopia, where it is relatively common in some areas and occurs on the edges of agricultural areas.

VAAL RHEBOK
(Pelea capreolus)

Many might argue about the inclusion of the vaal rhebok on a list of Africa's great trophies. I place it there for several reasons. It is a unique creature, occupying its own genus with just one species and one subspecies. It is confined to a limited range in South Africa's high country and, unlike most antelope, has defied all attempts to increase its tribe through game ranching; it occurs only in a natural state. More important, it is a beautiful little antelope, with a woolly coat and straight, sharp horns that appear incredibly long on its small frame. Perhaps most important, hunting it offers significant challenge, a genuine mountain hunt that is not uniformly successful.

Swarovski's Jim Morey took this excellent common waterbuck in South Africa. There is little visual difference among the various races of waterbuck, but a waterbuck with good horns is always a stunning trophy.

The vaal rhebok is found in suitable mountain habitat from the Cape mountains north through Orange Free State and into Natal. Nowhere is the animal particularly common, so hunting it is a matter of climbing, glassing, and usually long and difficult shooting. I rate it as the most challenging and interesting of South Africa's indigenous species, but you aren't obligated to agree.

We will next turn to my equally subjective list of what I think of as common game.

The big difference between what we think of "common game" and more prestigious prizes is that the animals in this group are more often taken through chance encounter rather than specifically hunted.

In most safaris it's the common game that feeds the camp, as well as providing bait animals for the cats. Almost all African antelope are superb table fare.

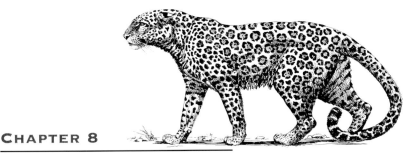

CHAPTER 8

"COMMON GAME" OFTEN ISN'T!

I don't like the term "common game." It belittles game animals that are beautiful and interesting in their own right—and it isn't always accurate. These animals are rarely primary goals—but that doesn't mean they're always easy! Depending on local conditions, any of the animals that we often think of as "common game" may be downright uncommon. How selective you wish to be is a factor, too. Most of the animals we're talking about here carry low trophy fees, are plentiful in many areas, and are often taken for camp meat and used as bait animals in cat hunting. This means that many are taken, so trophy standards are often quite high. Even if the animal is widespread and plentiful, it can be extremely difficult to find a really big one.

Plain old luck is always a factor, too—and can color the way you think about things. It is quite possible to take a big lion or a fine bongo on the first day of a safari. It is also quite possible to spend several days searching for a "common" animal such as a zebra or a hartebeest. The big difference to me isn't how easy or difficult a given animal is, or how plentiful it happens to be, because this can vary endlessly. The big difference is in the placement of priorities. A safari doesn't have to be successful to be wonderful, but most of the animals we have discussed in the last three chapters are, if not at the top, near the top of most hunters' wish lists on safaris in the areas where they occur. Failure to obtain any of them probably won't—and certainly shouldn't—prevent the safari from yielding fine memories. But if you come home without them you are likely to feel the hunting wasn't as successful as you wished it had been.

The "common game" we're talking about here is unlike those in the last three chapters. They may or may not be locally common, and they might also be spooky and difficult to approach. But they are unlikely to be near the top of any hunter's wish list, and few hunters will lose much sleep if they go home without them.

Most hunting areas hold several of the animals in this group, and in fact it is unusual for any given hunter to take all of the varieties of "common game" that are found in a given area. To some extent this is because they spend hunting days concentrating on animals that are a priority. It is also relatively difficult to locate a good specimen. For instance, most areas throughout Africa have warthogs, but a really good warthog is a scarce animal. Once again, "common" doesn't always mean "easy." Zebra are a good example of this. They are often extremely difficult to locate and even more difficult to approach. If you place priority on getting a zebra rug, you can usually obtain it, but there may be a limit on how many blown stalks you can make on zebra when you're spending your time tracking buffalo or looking for a big kudu.

This is all part of the wonderful world of safari. A given African area may hold somewhere between a dozen and twenty different varieties of game. Extensive game lists are enticing, but densities vary widely. Even on lengthy hunts you cannot effectively hunt them all, and you almost certainly will not collect them all. Some will come by chance encounter, some will come by specifically hunting a given animal, and some you won't encounter at all. It is true in some areas, such animals are plentiful enough that you can leave camp on a given morning and take an impala or a Grant gazelle, for example. But you may be so busy trying to find the animals you want most that you simply never get around to the others.

Except for very specialized safaris, such as for big elephant or bongo, under most circumstances you will take several varieties of the common game. They feed the camp, provide the baits, and also provide the spice that makes Africa so special—the incredible, never-ending variety of game that makes a safari the most wonderful experience in the hunting world.

When I think of common game I'm thinking of warthog and bushpig, zebra, impala, gazelle, hartebeest and other species of Damaliscus, wildebeest, and reedbuck. You don't have to agree with this list, nor do I under all circumstances. For instance, I'm going to Tanzania in September, and one of the animals that is very high on my list is a topi—simply because I have never before been in an area where topi occur. But under most circumstances none of these animals have such priority that hunters will spend a lot of time specifically pursuing them. We consistently judge the dainty gazelle beautiful, but we rarely describe wildebeest and warthog as beautiful. All are interesting, all can be challenging depending on the circumstances, and all add immeasurably to the experience that is Africa.

WARTHOG

(Phacochoerus aethiopicus)

Warthog are one of the most widespread of all African animals, occurring from Ethiopia to South Africa and across the continent to West Africa. They are common in some areas and quite scarce in others, and this can vary with the year. Warthog are prolific breeders, but they simply must have water. Under drought conditions warthog are among the first to go, and it takes several years for a male warthog to grow good tusks. Trophy quality remains poor for several years after a dry spell, even when numbers have rebuilt.

Although there are usually some warthog around, very few areas consistently produce good tusks. Ethiopia is famous for

127

producing huge warthog, but Zimbabwe and northern South Africa are also very good, at least partly due to well-developed water sources on game and cattle ranches.

The primary difficulty in hunting warthog lies in the fact that there is no predicting exactly where or when you might find a good one. It seems that on the rare occasions you do see a good warthog, you're hunting something else and are unwilling to take the shot. Priorities are important, but keep in mind that a really good warthog is extremely hard to come by, and if you see one you are unlikely to see it again!

Warthog are most active in the mornings and late afternoons, but they often go to water at midday. Still-hunting riverine cover in the early mornings and late evenings is always a good way to look for warthog. Watching a water hole through the midday hours is also a good bet. You never know what might turn up.

BUSHPIG
(Potamochoerus porcus)

If anything, bushpig are even more widespread than warthog, so I suppose they are technically "common game." The irony is that they are extremely nocturnal and prefer the densest bush imaginable. Hunters shoot some at night and take many through blind luck on a purely chance encounter, but there are few animals more difficult to hunt on purpose in the daylight. This is one of those animals that occurs on almost every game list and license list, and it isn't false advertising. Bushpig are almost certainly present, but few hunters will go home with one. I took one with dogs in the dense coastal thorn near Port Elizabeth, a fun hunt that was one of the most physically difficult hunting days I've ever spent. Over the course of more than thirty safaris in country where bushpig occur, I have seen them on exactly two occasions!

Although warthogs occur virtually throughout the length and breadth of Africa, really good boars are always scarce. The author took this one in Chad. A warthog was the farthest thing from his mind, but you don't pass tusks like these!

ZEBRA
(Equus buochelli)

Non-hunters (and a disturbing number of hunters) frequently ask, "How can you shoot a zebra?" The proper answer is, "Usually only with great difficulty." Few animals are as constantly alert as zebra, and few have a better combination of eyesight, hearing, and smell. There are several varieties, and some are truly great prizes. To my thinking Hartmann's mountain zebra should be a priority on any safari to Namibia, and hunting them on foot in their rocky habitat is a truly great hunt. One of my great regrets is that I never had the chance to take a Grevy zebra, the big-eared, pinstriped zebra of northern Kenya and Ethiopia, now fully protected wherever it occurs. Although the habitat changes, zebra are rarely easy to hunt.

Impala are found from Kenya southward and are very common in many areas. They are quite possibly the most recognizable of all African antelope, a beautiful little trophy.

In open plains it isn't difficult to glass for them, but in the heavy thornbush of southern Africa you will often track them just like buffalo. Either way, closing for a shot is usually a matter of tricky stalking. There is the added difficulty of picking out a stallion. This is not a legal requirement, nor is it a biological necessity, but it adds considerably to the challenge and makes the hunt all the more interesting. In brush you often cannot see the belly line, so you must judge the stallion by its thicker neck and, more important, by its behavior. Stalking a herd of zebra is a really fine hunting experience. Don't knock it 'till you've tried it!

IMPALA

(Aepyceros melampus)

The reddish-gold impala with its lyre-shaped horns is probably the most recognizable of all African antelope. It is beautiful, and its ability to run with great, leaping bounds is a wonderful sight to

The Grant gazelle is probably the most typical gazelle and one of the most widespread, occurring in several races from northern Tanzania to Ethiopia.

behold. The impala also provides some of Africa's best table fare. In impala country I reckon a safari hasn't really started until there are impala chops for supper and impala liver for breakfast!

The impala of East Africa are somewhat larger than the southern variety, and the black-faced impala of Angola and northern Namibia have distinctly different black facial markings. Still, there is just one species of impala, occurring generally from Kenya southward. The impala is a creature of mixed woodland and savanna. The dominant males tend to gather large harems, and the lesser males (not necessarily lesser in horn size) form bachelor herds. In many areas, including much of Zimbabwe, the northern Transvaal, Zambia's Luangwa Valley, and Tanzania's Selous Reserve, impala are by far the most numerous antelope, and it is possible to see hundreds in a given day.

In such areas, though not necessarily throughout them, you can say with conviction that you're going to get an impala, but it's not certain that you will get a good one. I tend to think the record-book minimums on impala are a bit low, because you can usually find a ram that will make the grade. But finding a really good one, a southern impala of perhaps twenty-four inches or an East African impala of twenty-seven inches, is extremely difficult. To some extent your success will depend on how much time you're willing to put into the effort. An inch or so of horn probably doesn't matter much, but no trophy room is complete without this most typical African antelope.

GAZELLE
(genera Antidorcas, Litocranius, and Gazella)

In the first genus, *Antidorcas marsupialis* is the springbok of southern Africa, also called a "pseudo-gazelle." Litocranius is the long-necked gerenuk found from northern Tanzania to Ethiopia, and Gazella are the true gazelles, ranging in many

Tracker Mahmoud and Ethiopian outfitter Colonel Negussie Eshete with a good northern gerenuk from the Danakil. The northern gerenuk is visually indistinguishable from the southern variety, but is bigger on the average in body and horn.

species and subspecies from northern Tanzania across North Africa and on east to China. Although the family is large, the habitat varies little. The gerenuk is exclusively a browser, found in arid thornbush, and the rest are both browsers and grazers, but all are found in relatively dry, open country.

This entire tribe is usually nervous and switched on. This is partly because their sharp eyes and fleet feet are their first line of defense against predators, but it is also due to hunting pressure. Stalking is difficult, shooting is usually far, and the target is small and rarely stands still for very long. Some of the animals in this group, such as the springbok and Grant gazelle, are properly common game. Others are important prizes, like the unique gerenuk and local rarities such as the red-fronted gazelle and the Soemmerring gazelle. The hunting is rarely easy and the shooting usually very difficult.

HARTEBEEST

(Alcelaphus buselaphus and related species of genus Damaliscus)

The former are the true hartebeests, divided into eight different record-book categories. The latter are a closely related group comprised of the similar korrigum, tiang, and topi; the sassaby; the Hunter antelope or hirola; and the bontebok and blesbok. They are all grazing antelope, usually found in fairly open country but ranging into woodlands as well as savanna and semi-desert. The various species, subspecies, and races are found discontinuously from north to south and east to west, so most hunting areas have one or another of these animals. Some varieties are localized; others inhabit a broad range.

A few of these two groups are considered significant prizes, but to some extent this is due to location. For example, the bontebok and the blesbok are strikingly similar, different primarily in color. The bontebok is an unusual purple from withers to hips, while the blesbok is much more drab. Unless

These are Thomson gazelles in the Great Rift Valley of northern Tanzania. There are dozens of races of gazelle, and most of them are fairly localized. They may be common where they occur, but you must go to a specific area to find them.

mounted life-size, it is extremely difficult to tell them apart in a trophy room. However, the bontebok population lay squarely alongside the Boer trekkers' advance, and by the beginning of the 1900s they were nearly extinct, with just a few individuals protected by farsighted farmers. Today they have increased to huntable numbers on quite a few South African game ranches, but supply is limited and trophy fees are high, so the bontebok is a desirable trophy, while the more plentiful, more widespread, and oh-so-similar blesbok is rarely considered so.

The korrigum, also called Senegal hartebeest (even though it is not a hartebeest and is no longer found in Senegal), ranges across Central Africa from Sudan westward. It is extremely plentiful in some areas and badly depleted in others. Hunting opportunities today are limited to remote areas such as C.A.R. and Chad, where safaris are expensive. The Hunter antelope (also called Hunter hartebeest) occupies a very limited range

134

The author, Chris Kinsey, and outfitter Alain Lefol with a korrigum from Chad.
The largest member of the genus Damaliscus, *korrigum (or Senegal hartebeest)*
were once very common but are now huntable only in very remote areas.

on the Kenya-Somalia border and is no longer hunted. The
tiang occupies a very broad range, but it happens to be in Sudan
and Uganda. The only current opportunity to hunt tiang is
in the Omo Valley of southwestern Ethiopia, where Nassos
Roussos hunts.

Some of the hartebeests are similarly localized, while others,
such as the Coke, lelwel, and Cape varieties, occupy fairly large
ranges. Although extremely fleet-footed, none of the animals
in this group is particularly wary, and they are all relatively easy
to hunt—most of the time. This depends on how plentiful they
happen to be in the area you are hunting, and also on the amount
of hunting pressure to which they have been subjected.
Bontebok are hunted very little and are notoriously placid, but
in the particular place I hunted them (and maybe on that
particular day) they were spooky as hell. In four trips to the
C.A.R. I never got a shot at a lelwel hartebeest, although tracks

showed there were some around. So you never know, but in most areas where hartebeest occur, a chance will come along.

WILDEBEEST
(Connochaetes gnou)

There are really just two species of wildebeest, the blue and the black. There are several different races of the blue wildebeest, or brindled gnu. Although the horns are all similar, they vary quite a bit in coloration. The blue wildebeest and its close cousins, Cookson wildebeest, Nyasa wildebeest, and white-bearded wildebeest, are found from Namibia northeast to Kenya. The significantly different black wildebeest (or white-tailed gnu) is found only in South Africa and was also introduced into Namibia.

Wildebeest are grazing antelope of open grasslands, often living in very large herds. They are famous for their annual migrations, following the rains that bring new grass, but not all populations migrate. If water is permanent they are more likely to be resident. Like any herd animal that lives in open country, wildebeest can be difficult to approach, but usually they are not. Compared with most African antelope they are not beautiful, but their rocking gait and comical antics are an important part of the African scene. Hunters tend to underestimate them. A big blue wildebeest bull can weigh five hundred pounds, and no African animal is tougher.

REEDBUCK
(Redunca redunca)

You could think of reedbuck as coming in sizes small, medium, and large. The small ones are the mountain reedbuck, the Chanler mountain variety, and the southern mountain reedbuck, which are separated by several thousand miles. The medium-size ones are the several races of bohor reedbuck, a small antelope averaging a bit under one hundred pounds.

They are more brightly colored than other reedbuck, ranging from yellow to reddish, and are found (in several subspecies) from Tanzania north to Ethiopia and across Central Africa to West Africa. The large variety is the common or southern mountain reedbuck, weighing about 150 pounds and occupying a broad range from Tanzania to South Africa.

Reedbuck are found in damp areas, and you will usually find them in the reeds or high grass. The mountain varieties are indeed found at high elevations, and I have seen Abyssinian bohor reedbuck up at eleven thousand feet with the mountain nyala. But you will generally not find reedbuck without water and patches of grass nearby. They are an attractive antelope, and their horns are not especially impressive but are unique in that the bases of the horns are surrounded by a soft, swollen mass that looks like, and is, new horn in the process of forming. Reedbuck are quite common in some areas and are darned difficult to find

Although common reedbuck are extremely widespread, it is unusual to see a really good one. This excellent buck was taken in Zambia's Kafue region.

elsewhere. The difficulty in hunting them usually depends on the local density; they can be very spooky, but they are extremely territorial. If you find a buck near a given patch of reeds, you can probably find it there again, even if you spook it.

Most African areas will hold some combination of the animals discussed herein. None hold them all. Even if they were all present, it's unlikely you would collect them all. Some you simply won't see; others you will see while you're busy hunting something else that holds a higher priority. You might even miss a couple of them. Over the course of a normal safari you will probably collect several of these animals—for camp meat, for bait, and also for trophies that will grace your walls and evoke fond memories for the rest of your life. Even if these animals are of high trophy quality, few will hold a place of honor alongside the dangerous game, the spiral horns, and the more glamorous antelope—but Africa simply wouldn't be Africa without them.

In our tour of Africa's principal game there's one important group missing: the little guys, the pygmy antelope. Africa wouldn't be Africa without them, either, and we'll take a look at them in the next chapter.

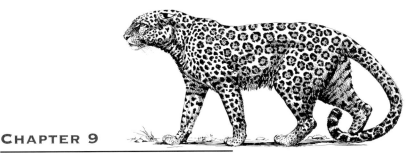

CHAPTER 9

BIG THINGS IN SMALL PACKAGES

The small antelope of Africa enrich what is already the world's greatest cornucopia of wildlife.

In previous chapters we have looked at Africa's Big Five; her spiral-horned antelope; a somewhat arbitrary selection of beautiful, high-profile trophies; and an equally arbitrary selection of the more common or less challenging animals. The picture is not complete without a discussion of Africa's small antelope. Encompassing dik-dik, duiker, and a broad range of other pygmy antelope—oribi, steenbok, grysbok, klipspringer, and more—this is an extensive collection of animals that is unique in the hunting world.

The small antelope differ widely in distribution and difficulty to hunt. Some of them, like bush duiker, dik-dik, steenbok, and oribi, will come along during the course of a normal safari in areas where they occur. Properly you might consider them common game, although they are only common where there are lots of them. Other game in this category, such as grysbok, suni, and most of the forest duikers, range between difficult and almost impossible to obtain. Some are widespread, some occupy specialized habitat (but are found nearly everywhere suitable habitat occurs), and many others are extremely localized.

Hunters also view the small antelopes in widely different ways. I must admit that I have never been particularly interested in them. Over the years I have taken a modest selection of the pygmy antelopes and duikers. Several have come through chance encounter, while others I worked darned hard to get a shot at. I have not always been successful. Although I've tried several times, I've never gotten a Cape grysbok. I'd like to have one, but it doesn't bother me much that I don't. I have a few forest duikers, but I've been in many areas that have varieties I haven't gotten. This doesn't bother me much, either. I would go back and hunt buffalo and any of the spiral horns again and again before I would mount a safari exclusively for any (or several) of the small antelopes. But every hunter has to establish his or her own priorities.

Quite a number of serious hunters really become intrigued by the small antelopes, making specialized forest hunts to Liberia and other parts of the forest zone for duikers and such. Others I have known have returned to South Africa with the express purpose of hunting suni, Natal red duiker, blue duiker, and Cape grysbok. I don't see myself planning a safari like either of these, not because it wouldn't be challenging. Many of the small antelope are extremely difficult to hunt. They are often very nocturnal, and are usually found in heavy bush or forest. By the way, it doesn't take much vegetation to hide an antelope the size of a jack rabbit!

If I don't hunt them, it's not because they're not beautiful. The duikers all have modest horns, but they occur in an incredible variety of sizes and colors and are extremely attractive as life-size mounts. The other pygmy antelopes and dik-diks are generally more drab in color, but are dainty, elegant, and equally attractive.

Some of the small antelope are legitimately counted among Africa's great prizes. These would include the tiny royal antelope, some of the more localized duikers of the deepest forests, and the dik-diks that are found only in the remotest areas. Come to think of it, excepting blind luck, very few of the small antelope could be considered easy to hunt. There is much truth in the old rhyme, "I'm going loony looking for a suni." I am pleased to have some of these animals among my own modest collection, and as time goes on I hope to add more varieties. However, I probably will not devote a large percentage of the African hunting days that remain to me in their pursuit. This is based entirely on personal preference and has nothing to do with beauty, merit, or challenge.

KLIPSPRINGER
(Oreotragus oreotragus)

Weighing around forty pounds, the "klippie" is one of the largest types of pygmy antelope. It is an attractive, stocky creature with stiff, varicolored hairs that, on close inspection, resemble quills. Its range is just plain weird: It is found discontinuously in rocky hill masses almost all over Africa, but there may be hundreds of miles between populations. Klipspringer offer a nice hunt because they are territorial where they occur, so if you go up a mountain that is known to hold them, chances are you will find them.

ORIBI
(Ourebia ourebia)

The oribi is another "large" animal in this group, running thirty-five to forty pounds and offering extremely tender, tasty venison. In my experience, where oribi occur they tend to be numerous, but they are not found in many areas. They occupy a broad but extremely discontinuous range; I have seen them in central C.A.R., in Zambia, and in Kenya, but do not recall seeing them anyplace else (although they do occur in many other areas). Oribi are creatures of grassy

The elegant oribi is one of the larger of the pygmy antelopes, occupying a huge but extremely discontinuous range. The author has seen oribi from South Africa to Chad, but on few occasions. This one was taken in Zambia's Bangweulu region.

plains, almost always found near water; if present, they are usually quite visible.

STEENBOK AND GRYSBOK
(Raphicerus campestris and R. melanotis)

Although steenbok and grysbok are closely related, they are significantly different in habit and habitat. The steenbok is an attractive little antelope with straight, sharp horns, weighing a bit over twenty pounds. It is a creature of dry, open plains and its habitat extends from East Africa southward. Unlike many of the pygmy antelope, the steenbok is most active during daylight hours, which means you might see it at any time of day. Hunters most often see and judge it and either take it or not while passing through its country or searching for more prestigious game; rarely is it specifically hunted. This is not meant to denigrate the steenbok. It is a very pretty little buck, and although it occupies a large range, good trophies are uncommon. I was fortunate to take a pretty good one on my first safari to Kenya many years ago. Although I have seen quite a few steenbok since, I have never, ever seen another good one. Its small size, coupled with open country habitat, means that your shot will probably be extremely difficult!

While steenbok are primarily grazers, their cousin, the grysbok, is primarily a browser. Their reddish-gold color is similar, but the grysbok has smaller horns and noticeably larger, more rounded ears. There are two grysbok: the Sharpe variety of the Zambezi and Limpopo drainages, and the Cape grysbok of South Africa's eastern Cape. The Sharpe grysbok is smaller than the steenbok, while the Cape grysbok is a bit larger. Both are primarily nocturnal creatures that spend their days in extremely thick brush. Getting a shot at either one is a solid challenge. Usually all you will see is a quick flash of a small, reddish antelope. If you can hit one with a rifle as it scurries to cover, you're a better man than I am. A problem equal to the shot itself is seeing the horns well enough to make a decision to shoot or not. There were quite a lot of Sharpe grysbok in the Zambezi Valley of Mozambique when I hunted elephant there in 1989, and I got one with little difficulty. Cape grysbok are another story. On several occasions I've hunted them quite hard, both day and night, and although I've seen quite a lot of them, I've never seen one for long enough to put horns on its head. Because of their brush-loving, nocturnal nature, grysbok are usually specifically hunted—but the chances for success are not great unless you invest a lot of time in the effort.

SUNI AND ROYAL ANTELOPE
(Neotragus moschatus and N. pygmaeus)

Oh, boy, now we're into the tough stuff! There are three types of suni. The Livingstone suni is found in the dense coastal

Dik-dik are relatively common in East Africa's dry thornbush, and you'll often see them darting off into the brush. It may take a little while, but usually one will stop in a spot open enough to see the horns. This is a good Kirk dik-dik, taken in southern Kenya.

vegetation along the Indian Ocean coastline of southern Africa. Weighing as much as fifteen pounds, it is the largest of this group. The East African suni is smaller, weighing about ten pounds, and is found in similar habitat but also at higher elevations in the mountains of Kenya and Tanzania. The royal antelope is found on the other side of the continent, in the dense forests of coastal West Africa. It is Africa's smallest-hoofed animal and, excepting the Asian mouse deer, the smallest in the world at about five pounds. All three are browsing animals, primarily nocturnal; their small size, coupled with the incredibly thick foliage they inhabit, makes them among Africa's most difficult prizes. Relatively few hunters have taken a suni, fewer still both varieties—and in the history of African hunting only a handful of sportsmen have taken royal antelope.

Suni and royal antelope will respond to the same sort of mewing call that is used to lure forest duikers. The difficulty is much the same: seeing the animal well enough (and for long enough) to distinguish male from female. This problem is compounded by the very small size of these animals, and the fact that genuine concentrations of any of them are rare. Newly reopened Liberia probably offers the only chance for royal antelope. Although a bag in that country will probably include several different varieties of forest duiker, chances for a royal antelope are slim. It is best to hunt East African suni in conjunction with Abbott duiker in the thick forest of Tanzania's mountains. Zululand is probably the best place to hunt Livingstone suni today. Given enough time in the right area, both varieties of suni are attainable—but don't make any bets on a royal antelope!

DIK-DIK

(Madoqua saltiana/M.guentheri/M. kirki...)

The dik-diks are small antelope of dry thornbush, weighing around ten pounds, with very short, sharp, cylindrical horns. They are divided into four species and ten races or subspecies, essentially ranging the East African plains and semi-deserts from the Red Sea Hills south to northern Tanzania, with the exception of the Damara dik-dik of Namibia and Angola. Some of the races are localized, while others, like the Damara dik-dik and the Kirk dik-dik of Kenya and northern Tanzania, occupy a fairly broad range. Either way, they are rarely specifically hunted but, because they occupy fairly open country, hunters usually encounter them when hunting in their habitat. They may mate for life and are usually seen in pairs, so if you see a female take a good look around—the little buck is probably nearby.

As with most of the small antelope, a hunter's greatest difficulty is seeing the horns. This is especially difficult on dik-dik because a tuft of long hair between the ears not only obscures the horns on smaller males but at first glance makes a female appear as if she has horns. Fortunately, dik-dik live in fairly open country, so you can often use binoculars on a

The pretty red-flanked duiker is the only member of this large group that is fairly consistently seen on the edges of the forest rather than in the forest itself.

stationary animal, instead of getting a quick glimpse at a tiny form darting for cover!

BUSH (COMMON) DUIKER
(Sylvicapra grimmia)

Bush duikers are found in woodland and thornbush habitat literally throughout Africa. For record-keeping purposes we have divided them into several regional categories, but they are visually indistinguishable, except that the southern bush duiker, weighing up to forty pounds, is significantly larger than the races found farther north. They are all grayish-brown or brownish-gray, with short, round, fairly thick horns and a longish face. Browsing antelope, they are mostly nocturnal, often seen along the edges of wooded areas in early morning and late afternoon. The bush duikers are usually considered common game. They are usually not specifically hunted, but in most areas they are plentiful enough to be encountered in the course of a normal safari.

FOREST DUIKER
(Cephalophus monodical/C. maxmelli/C. rufilatus...)

The forest duikers are a huge and diverse group, ranging in size from the tiny blue duiker, less than ten pounds, to the Jentink duiker, weighing nearly two hundred pounds. Obviously, a two-hundred-pound animal is not "small." There are two other large duikers: the yellow-backed, which weighs up to 150 pounds, and the Abbott, weighing perhaps one hundred pounds. With these exceptions, most of the many varieties of forest duiker range from about twenty to forty pounds. They also vary dramatically in color and range, with many varieties extremely localized and others occupying a broad range. They are all primarily nocturnal and are mostly

147

Few hunters go in search of the various bush duikers, but you must be where they occur in order to take one. This is a West African bush duiker from C.A.R.

found in the thickest forest. The one consistent exception to this is the red-flanked duiker, which is usually found not in the forest but along the edges of the thick stuff.

The record book recognizes nearly twenty different varieties of forest duiker, based primarily on size and color. Because of the duikers' secretive nature, and ranges that are often localized and usually confined to nearly impenetrable forest, it is extremely unlikely that we have yet identified all the races of forest duiker. It is possible that we have not even encountered all of them. South Africa has localized populations of blue duiker, and the Natal red duiker is found in dense vegetation along the Indian Ocean coast. Farther north there are a few varieties of forest duiker in similar coastal forest and also on the forested slopes of East Africa's mountains. The yellow-backed duiker, although almost never

The yellow-backed duiker is one of the three giant duikers. At about 140 pounds, it is considerably larger than Abbott duiker and smaller than Jentink. Professional hunter Jacques Lemaux called this one in eastern C.A.R.

common, occupies a broad range that extends down through Zaire and into Zambia and Angola. However, the true forest zone of Central and West Africa is the real treasure trove of forest duikers.

Most forest areas, whether in southern C.A.R., southern Cameroon, or Congo, will have at least three or four varieties of forest duiker. Usually these include the little blue duikers and the big yellow-backs, with more localized varieties in-between. The forests of West Africa may hold a half-dozen varieties, and indeed this is the primary attraction in Liberia. What we think of as "big game" is scarce there, but the variety of duikers is unlimited.

While walking through the forest it is always possible to encounter virtually any type of duiker that happens to occur where you are, but the prospects for a chance encounter resulting in a good shot are quite slim. Calling affords by far the best opportunity and is also an exciting and interesting way to hunt. I believe at least some duikers would probably respond to a good old American varmint call, but the African trackers call by making a plaintive, nasal, mewing sound deep in their throats. I'm not sure whether the response is curiosity or an instinctive response to one of their own in trouble, but the forest duikers will come to such a sound.

Sometimes they come tentatively; you just hear a faint scratching of leaves and you strain to see the animal through the leaves. Other times they charge the call—twice I've been nearly run over by yellow-backed duikers. You never know exactly what might come in; it might be any of the local varieties of duiker, or it might be something else. In C.A.R. I've seen bushbuck, bushpig, and one very big leopard come in while I was attempting to call duiker! As I said at the beginning, this type of game is not my personal priority, but the calling is fascinating. I've spent late afternoons calling duiker while on bongo and Derby eland safaris. In Liberia hunters do much of their calling at night. Darkness compounds the basic problem of identifying the animal that has come to the call and then trying to see the horns. It is a most interesting game, and I can fully understand why some otherwise rational people get totally hooked on it!

OTHER SMALL GAME

Throughout Africa, there is a great variety of other animals that are usually not considered "big game" but that are an important part of the ecosystem. These include the canines—hyenas, jackals, and wild dogs; smaller cats (although they aren't all true cats)—servals, civets, genets, and lynxes; baboons and monkeys; and just plain "varmints" like rock hyraxes and springhares. Depending on the area, some of these animals

Chris Kinsey and the author admire a couple of knob-billed geese taken in wetlands near N'Djamena, Chad.

are on license, some are fully protected, and others are completely unprotected. Hunters can effectively call the smaller predators and often can hunt them at night. My hunting buddy, Joe Bishop, is one of many hunters who really likes to collect the smaller animals, and he has put them to good use. Accenting his excellent collection of great prizes in his trophy room are wonderful life-size genets, civets, springhares, and the like.

BIRD HUNTING

At least some bird hunting is available in most areas, and some areas are fabulous. Bird safaris are relatively common in Botswana and are becoming more so in South Africa, Zimbabwe, and Namibia. Africa's bird life is rich and varied, and her game birds are no less numerous than her songbirds and shorebirds. On a normal big-game safari, few hunters will devote exclusive hunting days to wingshooting, but there is usually time if you want to sample it. There are afternoons when a buffalo track doesn't work out, "days off" after taking a major animal, and so forth. An afternoon at a water hole when the sand grouse are coming in is

The smaller predators are mostly nocturnal and thus not easy to hunt, but they make excellent additions to any trophy room. This is a big civet cat with an unusually well-marked skin.

wonderful, and there is no better table fare than the many varieties of francolin. I like to hunt guinea fowl, something like our desert quail; it's usually a footrace to get them to fly, but they fly just fine when they get airborne! The wonderful thing about African hunting is there is no such thing as "dead time." Whether it's calling duiker, searching futilely for suni or grysbok, shooting birds, or calling small predators, exciting hunting is always close at hand.

Rifle or Shotgun?

Keen bird hunters may wish to bring a favorite bird gun—and make sure your outfitter lays in some shells of the proper gauge. The question whether to use a rifle or a shotgun relates to the best choice for the small antelopes. In open country, where dik-diks may be found, a rifle is clearly the right choice—and if you're shooting a normal centerfire rifle, solids

There are wetlands in Africa that often hold a wealth of waterfowl. The author rarely brings his own shotgun, but there's usually a camp gun around. The problem is that a short-barreled shotgun like this Benelli, intended as backup for leopard, isn't much of a goose gun!

are the obvious choice to avoid undue damage. When calling in the forest the right choice is less clear. We were once calling for blue duiker, and I had a .22 rimfire in my hands the afternoon the leopard came in! Overall, I think a shotgun loaded with relatively fine buckshot is probably the best choice for calling in the thick stuff; under these circumstances the precision of a rifle is not called for and may be counterproductive. On the other hand, the day I got my yellow-backed duiker it charged the call, then hung up in some thick stuff just at the limit of our vision. I had my .375 in my hands, but the duiker was out of reach of a buckshot-loaded shotgun. So I'm not sure there's a best solution. Whether you're holding a .22, a shotgun, or a scoped centerfire, sometimes you'll be right and sometimes you'll be wrong. As with all hunting situations, you have to roll the dice and do the best you can with the shot you're given, or pass it up and wait for a better opportunity. In chapter 13, I'll discuss in detail how to select the right guns to take with you.

This concludes our brief look at Africa's game and game country. In the next chapter we'll get down to the basics of planning your safari, starting with a look at the many options available in modern hunting safaris.

PART III

PLANNING YOUR SAFARI

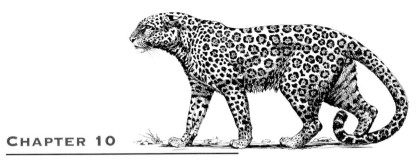

CHAPTER 10

THE MODERN SAFARI

Today's safaris come in many shapes and sizes, and I can't imagine an African hunt that isn't wonderful. But modern safaris are not the same as they were fifty years ago. Today's safaris tend to be short and fast-paced. The secret is to understand the range of options available and decide what is best for you.

I hope that we have all read Robert Ruark's *Horn of the Hunter*. It was that book, more than any other factor, that sparked my desire to go to Africa. It stands as the very best account of a single safari—a lengthy safari to Tanganyika nearly fifty years ago. If you haven't read it, do. It will make you want to go to Africa (or go there again). The Africa Ruark described is still there, waiting for you. But the safari he described is a piece of history, and you cannot base your expectations on it.

Let's take a closer look at the modern safari. The driving factors in choosing safaris are usually some combination of desired game, available time, and budget. But you shouldn't lose sight of the fact that a safari is supposed to be fun. How much fun it will be depends on how well it meets your expectations. Unfortunately, we often base our expectations on what we've read, and most of the good stuff is seriously outdated—which doesn't take long in Africa!

SHORT AND SHORTER

That pretty much describes the modern safari. Theodore Roosevelt's 1909 safari lasted some nine months.

Ethiopia offered some of the last "go anywhere" safaris. In 1993 Joe Bishop and the author finished in the mountains and headed for Asela, where Joe took this fabulous Menelik bushbuck; then they went on to the Danakil for gerenuk, oryx, and other game. The rules are different today, and camp changes must be planned in advance.

That was unusually long even for his day, but clear into the 1950s many safaris lasted two or three months, and a thirty-day safari was considered short. It's a busy world we live in these days, and time is the most precious commodity for many successful people. Today a thirty-day safari is rare, and three weeks is considered long. It's my guess that the modern hunting safari averages about ten days, and one-week hunts are more common than two-week hunts.

There's nothing wrong with this; it's just a function of the increasingly busy world we live in. Fortunately, thanks to jet aircraft that get you to Africa and light planes that whisk you to camp, it takes far less time than ever before to leave your home in the United States and be hunting in Africa. Actually, depending on the circumstances, I can be hunting in Africa in

There are some mobile safaris remaining. Alain Lefol's concessions in Chad total 25 million acres; in 2001 the author used Cabela's tents, changing camps five times. This is a rare situation today, when Chad's remaining game lie in pockets a long distance apart.

less travel time than it takes to get to remote areas in Canada or Alaska. That's the good news.

The bad news is that Africa's game animals really don't care how tight your schedule is. Part of the rationale for the longer safaris of yesteryear was that it actually takes a long time to have a good chance to bag some of the more elusive or locally rare species. Note that there isn't necessarily more game today than there was a half-century ago, though in some cases game actually is more plentiful. Thanks to game ranching— which means permanent water, agriculture, and the resulting ideal "edge" habitat—a seven- or ten-day "ranch" safari can produce results that match or rival much longer safaris of years ago, in terms of both trophy quality and species bagged. On the other hand, with difficult animals such as the cats, elusive antelope like bongo and Derby eland, and big elephant, the

Permanent camps in established hunting concessions are a far cry from the last generation's safaris, but the camps are comfortable and the game is usually plentiful and well protected. This is Alain Lefol's headquarters in southeastern C.A.R.

more time you have the better off you are. It simply isn't fair to compare the results of a three-week safari with a safari lasting three months. This is especially true in these times, when there might be more leopard but there are far fewer well-maned lion and large-tusked elephant.

CONCESSIONS

There was a time when a safari could travel the length and breadth of an entire country. There were few people, few cattle, and few safaris. A professional hunter, based on his knowledge of the country and his ability to get there, could take his clients to the very best places for certain game. They could hunt for a time and then go off to a place that was best for other game. This freewheeling hunting has never been common in southern Africa.

Outfitters are usually obligated to use as much of the quota as possible, so shorter hunts for high-quota animals like buffalo can be real bargains. Art Wheaton, Cliff Walker (the PH), and the author with a good Tanzanian buffalo taken in the Selous Game Reserve on a short buffalo hunt in 2000.

The temporary closure of Tanzania and the permanent closure of Kenya in the 1970s ended it in East Africa. I could be wrong, but my belief is that the last opportunity for a safari that could go anywhere and hunt any legal game ended with Ethiopia's most recent closure in 1993. When she reopened in '98 she followed the rest of the continent in allocating exclusive outfitter concessions.

I am aware of only one truly mobile, far-ranging safari offered today, and it is in Chad. In January 2001 my hunting partner, Chris Kinsey, and I roamed across five hundred miles of Africa with outfitter Alain Lefol, moving our camp about six times. The game was specialized—Barbary sheep and Dorcas gazelle in the north, western greater kudu in the center, and Senegal hartebeest and red-fronted gazelle in the south. It was a marvelous experience but, in today's Africa, a most unusual experience.

Exclusive concessions are not a bad thing. A given outfitter is assigned a certain piece of country, and he bids on or purchases the hunting rights to that area. This means that he has no competition from other safaris within that area. Usually this means that he is charged, to a greater or lesser degree, with managing the game within that area. Even if he is not, it is clearly in his own best interests to curtail poaching, manage meat hunting, improve the habitat (by developing permanent water, for instance), and maintain a harvest that ensures continuing trophy quality. Another positive aspect is that the outfitter becomes extremely familiar with his area. Over time he learns where certain species are most likely to be, and during which months. If the concession is long-term, it is worth his investment to develop permanent camps that are more comfortable and less expensive to maintain in the long run.

A dozen years ago the author took this lion as a wonderful bonus on a hunt in Tanzania. These days, with ever-shrinking quotas, it is extremely rare to be able to take the more prized species unless you have specifically arranged to hunt them.

The primary limitation is that no given concession is big enough to offer all the species a given country might have, or to offer the trophy quality modern clients desire. A good example is the wonderful Loliondo area long held by Cotton Gordon. Right on the edge of the Serengeti, it's one of the best lion areas in Africa—but, even though it is technically still Masailand, it's too far west to hold some of the principal Masailand species, such as lesser kudu. Or, in Zambia, a Kafue concession will not hold puku or Cookson wildebeest, and even the best Luangwa concession cannot offer sable or Crawshay waterbuck. In addition, all concessions are finite. Some are huge, others are large, and some are relatively small—but even if the available acreage is large, there are only so many places you can look for a given species of game. If drought or too much rainfall has caused a given animal population to move elsewhere, you may not be able to do anything about it.

To some extent, this means that you should plan your safari around a certain concession. This is almost as important as selecting an outfitter or professional hunter. For example, the best lion hunter in the world can't help you if he doesn't have access to a good lion area. This level of detail is sometimes difficult to winnow out when sorting through all the hype surrounding the sale of a safari, but it's critical, especially with the really hard-to-get species. Mind you, some outfitters have multiple concessions and some do not. But even if an outfitter holds multiple concessions, that doesn't necessarily mean you can move if things aren't going right. Switching to another area may be logistically difficult or even prohibitive, and even though the animal you seek may be found there, that doesn't mean the quota is available.

Making Quota

Game quotas are a relatively new thing in Africa. In general, a quota means that only a certain number of animals

One advantage to the quota system is that there are often "bonuses" toward the end of the season. The author's buddy, Pete Traphagen, was able to take this excellent Livingstone eland in the Zambezi Valley, where eland are on quota but scarce enough that it's hard to figure who will run into one.

of a given species may be taken within a given area. This is a good thing, because it ensures continued trophy quality for the future. Purely from a management standpoint, I can't think of a single thing wrong with a carefully derived and sensible quota. But it is a reflection of modern hunting, with a finite supply of game and a seemingly infinite demand.

Some quotas, especially on private lands, are inflicted by the landowners. The game departments enact most quotas, and they are essentially a condition for tendering a concession. Game departments rarely establish a quota with perfect knowledge of a game population, so some quotas are too high and others are too low. From a management standpoint, the former is a disaster, while the latter means exceptionally good hunting but usually difficult booking and higher prices.

The quota is a fact of life in today's Africa. What it really means is that there are few "extras" on the modern safari. Sure,

In 1994 Geoff Broom organized a mobile camp so the author's party could explore some new country far up the Ugalla River in Tanzania. The idea is romantic, but whenever you change camp you're going to lose some valuable hunting days.

late in the season there may be leftover quota that you can take advantage of, but don't count on it. These days, when booking a safari, you must be very specific about the game you wish to hunt, including the primary species, the secondary trophies, and even the bait animals. If you don't specify a given animal—even a relatively common animal—there may not be quota available.

Increasingly, African countries are requiring that license fees be paid "up front." We expect this on any North American hunt, but it's hard to deal with in Africa, where you simply don't know what you might encounter. Zambia is a good example of this system, and Ethiopia is another. Since you must buy licenses up front, you have to guess as best you can which animals you will encounter. You should concentrate on the animals that are of greatest interest to you, whether or not you really think you will encounter them. Botswana is a special situation, because today's quotas are so limited that you must usually specify species upon booking, even if the book is a couple of years ahead.

Sometimes this is all to the good. I hear stories about hunters who booked for certain animals but wound up taking some spectacular "other trophies" because quota happened to be available while they were there. This has never happened to me. I've been caught up in the quota question, but only in negative ways. On my first trip to Botswana, back in 1985, I couldn't have a red lechwe because the quota was full and I didn't mention it up front. In 2000 I went into Ethiopia's mountains with only mountain nyala and warthog licenses. I would have loved to take an Abyssinian bohor reedbuck, but there was only one on quota, even though we saw many. My partner took the one license and got a good one.

Really reputable outfitters allocate their quotas with honesty and diligence, but professional hunters are not bookkeepers. The message should be clear: These days you must specify all the game you would like to hunt, and get quota availability in writing at the time of booking. Maybe you'll get a bonus, but first you must ensure that the game you desire most can be hunted. Quotas are increasingly tight these days, so there are very few multiples of any given species—and you can expect bait animals to count against your license.

SWITCHING AREAS

Most outfitters have more than one area to hunt, and very large concessions may have several camps within a single concession. The outfitter may have added new areas or camps simply to expand operations, and these will probably offer opportunity to hunt other types of game. By moving camps you can expand the amount and type of game available during a single safari. For instance, in Tanzania it is relatively common to split a safari between a Masailand block—where the "East African" species (gazelle, lesser kudu, and the like) can be hunted—and a concession farther south or west, where "southern game" (sable, roan, and sitatunga) can be found. In Zambia it's common to spend a few days in Bangweulu for lechwe and sitatunga, while the bulk of the safari is spent in a Kafue or Luangwa block. Even in the context of a short plains-game safari, it is quite common to switch areas. In South Africa's eastern Cape it is common to hunt the mountains for vaal rhebok, a Karroo area for springbok and gemsbok, and somewhere else for kudu and the like.

I'm not at all opposed to switching areas; I have actually done relatively few safaris that stay in one area for the duration. However, you must understand that moving takes time and often money. Outfitters vary widely in how they allocate "hunting days." Sometimes a "fourteen-day safari" is inclusive of arrival and departure, really meaning twelve hunting days, and sometimes it is exclusive, meaning fourteen actual hunting days. Either is fine, so long as you understand the arrangement up front. Travel days within a safari are almost always lost hunting days. If a charter airplane is required, the cost can be considerable and there will be little flexibility. There may be little flexibility in any event; the logistics required to move from one area to another may need to be set up too far in advance to permit a change of plans. Usually there is more flexibility if you can drive from one area to another. It will also be less costly, but you will lose more time, meaning loss of valuable hunting days. Also, you can let yourself in for some long, tough days on the road. In Africa the actual distance is often secondary to the condition of the roads. An area shift may not look far on a map, but it can mean an extremely long day or two days of slow progress over potholed, rutted, or even washed-out roads.

Roads remain poor in much of Africa, so light aircraft offer the fastest way to change areas. Beware: Charter costs are extremely high in Africa, and moving around can add exponentially to the safari cost.

The most important consideration in switching areas, however, should not be the cost or the time but the potential impact on what is most important to you. If your primary desire is to see as much country as possible and obtain the widest range of game within a country or a given outfitter's concessions, then you probably have to do some moving around. Your safari will not be as leisurely, and you will probably leave some business undone in almost every area you visit. It is difficult to hunt animals like lion and leopard on a tight schedule; difficult antelope like sitatunga, eland, and bongo also take time. If you put yourself in a time crunch, almost any animal may be difficult to find in the time you have allocated. Moving around also adds pressure. The more leisurely the pace and the less rushing around you do, the more enjoyable your safari will be.

PLAINS-GAME SAFARIS

Most safaris of ten days or less will be safaris for a variety of plains game. Even a short safari doesn't necessarily imply that you will stay in one area, but the areas probably will not be very far apart. It is common in South Africa to hunt one ranch for a couple of species, then hunt another ranch for game that occurs there in better trophy quality. You may be able to do this from one camp; other times it is necessary to stay overnight. Short plains-game safaris are a specialty of southern Africa, and they are the most common safari in South Africa, Namibia, and Zimbabwe. These are fun hunts; costs are low, there is little pressure, and you can expect a good selection of plains game. Anticipate about one trophy per one-and-a-half hunting days.

"PLAINS GAME AND . . ."

The next tier of safaris is usually plains game plus either buffalo or leopard. To my mind, if affordable, a "plains game and buffalo" safari is the ideal first safari. Costs are higher than for a simple plains-game safari, and on a ten-day hunt of this type the bag of plains game will probably be smaller. But I'm real high on the wonderful experience that a buffalo hunt offers, and you can usually hunt for buffalo hunting in conjunction with a variety of plains game. This type of hunt is available primarily in Zimbabwe, Zambia, and Tanzania.

With leopard on the increase, ten- and fourteen-day "leopard and plains game" hunts are also very common, and may actually be less expensive than a "buffalo and plains-game" hunt. The pitfall is that, unless you are lucky, the leopard is usually time-consuming to hunt and requires concentrated effort. If leopard is the main quarry, then you really should concentrate on leopard. It may require all of your hunting days and may not end in success. I do not believe a leopard hunt makes a good first safari, but such a hunt is excellent for a second or third trip.

Satellite communications are gradually replacing the old radios throughout Africa. No matter how remote the area, these days there is usually some "reachback" to civilization in case of emergency.

GENERAL-BAG SAFARIS

These are the safaris that used to be about thirty days in duration. Today they are most likely to be two to three weeks. To me the most important characteristic is not time but the availability of multiple animals in the Big Five—for example, lion and buffalo, leopard and buffalo, both cats and buffalo. Such safaris are available in Botswana, Zimbabwe, Zambia, Tanzania, Cameroon, and C.A.R. If the lion is important on such a hunt, then you need to give it as much time as possible. Fourteen days in one area is the minimum I would recommend, and still there are no guarantees. On a three-week hunt you could reasonably spend a week in one area and two weeks in another. However, if you're really serious about both cats on one safari, then it is far better not to worry about a wide selection of plains game and to spend the whole three weeks on just one area.

Specialized Safaris

These are lengthy hunts for just one great prize. The hunter expects little else along the way, at least until he takes the major prize—and even then there may not be a lot of other game available. A lion or leopard hunt can be very specialized, especially if you've tried a couple of times before and failed! Elephant hunting is almost always a single-minded pursuit, except in Botswana and the Selous Reserve, where you may hunt a variety of other game. The really difficult antelope—bongo, Derby eland, and mountain nyala—are almost always approached as specialized endeavors. The best way to hunt these animals is to really concentrate on them for two or, better, three weeks. These hunts are best for experienced hunters; if you get sidetracked by other game you are hurting your chances for success on the primary prize. While these safaris aren't "shoot 'em ups" with big bags, one very good thing about them is that the pace is usually a bit slower, and they offer a pure hunting experience.

Multiple Countries

I don't know why more hunters don't exercise the option of hunting two or three countries. It is quite possible to hunt any combination of Zimbabwe, Namibia, and South Africa on a single overseas plane ticket. Internal connections and road networks are good, so, with good planning, you lose relatively little hunting time in transfers. The downside is that there's lots of rushing around and the planning is much more complicated; most of the time this involves separate short hunts with separate, unconnected outfitters. It is possible to do this type of hunt on a grand scale. A friend of mine, Neil Gibson, hunted lion, leopard, and buffalo in Zambia, then moved to Zimbabwe and hunted elephant, and finished up in South Africa with a white rhino hunt! More often, however, hunters do this to expand the range of key plains game. For instance, they hunt nyala in South Africa, gemsbok in Namibia, sable in Zimbabwe. Quota is increasingly limited today, so it is difficult to find outfitters who can allow you to hunt key species such as sable and nyala on short hunts. Multi-country safaris are a good way to maximize your time, not only increasing your bag but allowing you to see a lot more of Africa in a short period. I have done this several times, and, although the pace is not leisurely, I like the option. For me, it actually differs little from simply switching areas within a country, because these days it is quite common for the professional hunter and camp staff to stay in one area while only the client makes the shift.

That's what the modern safari looks like. It is usually fast-paced and frenetic, especially if you visit multiple areas within the framework of today's short safari. Success is usually fabulous, a tribute to today's professional hunters, who have adjusted to their clients' increasingly tight schedules. In the next chapter we will look at the basic decisions you must make at the very beginning of the planning process.

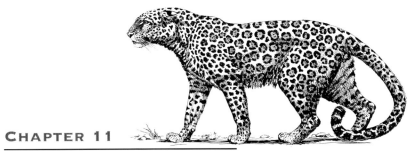

CHAPTER 11

BASIC DECISIONS

If you don't know what you want, how can anyone help you?

"I want to hunt Africa." That's a statement I frequently hear at hunters' conventions. I like to hear it, because the more people interested in African hunting, the healthier the safari industry. And if people weren't interested in African hunting, I couldn't write about it, now could I? Now don't take this wrong, but "I want to hunt Africa" is a ridiculous and almost meaningless statement.

Look at it this way: The African continent is so large that the United States would fit into it more than six times. I have never heard anyone say, "I want to hunt the United States." No. One might say, "I want to hunt the Rocky Mountains," or, more specifically, "I want to hunt elk (or mule deer, or sheep, or whatever)." For many of us Africa is beyond our comfort zone of knowledge, and the tendency is to lump it all into the same mental picture.

In previous chapters I tried to help out, first by discussing the various types of habitat you might encounter, and then by giving a brief rundown on the major classes of African game. It is important to know not only what the various types of game are but where they are found. Some people simply want to "hunt Africa," with little regard for the specific animals they may encounter or the type of country in which they may encounter them. Most hunters, however, plan safaris in the hope of encountering a few specific animals.

It's a lot easier to help someone if he or she says: "I want to hunt Cape buffalo." Now we can tie the safari to the several

In most cases your decision about where to hunt will be based on the game that is most important to you. Many first-timers want buffalo as part of the bag, and there are several good options. This bull was taken in Zimbabwe, one of the most economical destinations for a buffalo safari.

countries that offer buffalo hunting. When you investigate a little further you will usually discover that the wish list extends beyond just buffalo. Most people also want some of the "trimmings" along with their buffalo: kudu, impala, zebra. No problem; there are still lots of options. Sometimes I run into folks whose wish list just goes on and on. They often mention sable. Still no problem; you could combine sable with buffalo and kudu and such in Zimbabwe, Zambia, or Tanzania, but your safari will probably not be short, nor will it be inexpensive. Then they bring up gemsbok, and we're out of business. Gemsbok don't occur where sable and buffalo occur. You might as well throw in bongo and giant eland, and we're right back to "Let's hunt Africa!"

The type of game you wish to hunt is an extremely important consideration in planning a safari—for many of us, the overriding concern. If specific types of game are important to you, then you need to acquire a working knowledge of where Africa's principal species occur, and where they are best hunted. Previous chapters in this book are a good start, but I would advise further reading. You also need to establish reasonable goals based primarily on the time and money you can spend on your safari. So let's look at the basic decisions you need to make. It's better to make them before you start shopping.

WHAT DO YOU WANT TO HUNT?

To some extent the type of game you have in mind will determine where to focus your shopping. You can hunt buffalo in lots of places—darn near anywhere except Namibia. If you're looking for kudu, any of the southern African countries will work. Your options are more limited when you want certain animals in combination. Except for those who plan specialized safaris for the real rarities, most of us have a wish list several animals deep. This is perfectly fine. Part of the charm of Africa is her rich variety of wildlife, and most of us are looking for several different trophies, especially on our first few safaris.

It is important to decide what animals interest you in addition to your primary quarry. For instance, if a good buffalo is the main course and you don't much care what side dishes come with it, then a short hunt in Tanzania may be perfect. You will have two buffalo on license, and you can also hunt a selection of common game—hartebeest, wildebeest, zebra, impala, and so forth. However, many hunters want a kudu in addition to the buffalo. That would rule out Tanzania, because kudu are only available on a twenty-one-day license, as are sable. You would need to focus on southern Africa, probably Zimbabwe, but possibly South Africa or Mozambique.

The author gets a lot of mail asking about combining gemsbok with buffalo and/or sable. This is a tough combo, because gemsbok are primarily desert animals, while buffalo and sable are creatures of thornbush and woodland.

Sable is another high-profile animal that ranks high on the "wish list." Unless you are taking a lengthy and costly safari, Zimbabwe—where sable can easily be combined with both buffalo and kudu—is probably the best bet.

Obviously, you should base your choice of country and area primarily on the availability of the top two or three animals on your wish list. It is also wise to decide what else you might like to hunt. This is important in planning your trophy fee budget, and you should go over your wish list with your outfitter or his agent when you book the hunt. Some countries require that licenses be purchased "up front," and even if this is not the case, most areas do have a limited quota on almost all species. If you don't say anything about an animal you would like to hunt, there is no guarantee you'll have quota available.

How Long Can You Hunt?

That old saying "time is money" was never truer. The daily rate—your outfitter's fee—will probably be the largest single cost of your safari. This means the length of your safari will be dictated not only by how much time you have, but also by how much you want to spend. Many of us are driven to short hunts purely by budgetary constraints, and there isn't anything to be done about that. Just remember that the amount of hunting—and the size of your trophy shipment—are determined by the length of time you can hunt.

While it's good to get straight in your mind the game you might like to hunt, don't get all wrapped up in an extensive shopping list. The more hunting time you have, the longer your list can be and the more selective you can be in filling it. But unless your list is quite short, it's unlikely you'll get a chance at every animal on it. All outfitters have lists of available game. Most areas have at least ten different varieties, and some have more than twenty. Regardless of how extensive the list, don't expect that you'll bag every single animal that occurs in your area. If you select your area and outfitter well and concentrate your efforts, you will probably get your major trophy and some of the secondary trophies you would like.

Bob Maschmedt took this leopard on a relatively short hunt while the rest of the hunters spent their time hunting buffalo. It takes a fair amount of luck to get either lion or leopard in less than two weeks. Even then there's no guarantee, but if you are willing to concentrate your efforts your chances are much better.

You won't get them all, but you might well get one or two animals you hadn't thought about.

A couple of years ago my buddy Pete Traphagen made his first safari, hunting with Doug Carlisle in Russ Broom's Zambezi Valley area. Pete got a good buffalo and a fine kudu, his two primary trophies. Also on his list was a zebra, which he did not get, but he got a super Livingstone eland, an animal he hadn't considered hunting. Africa is like that; you never know exactly what you might encounter. It is extremely unlikely that you'll see trophy specimens of every single animal in which you are interested, especially in the early stages of your African hunting career, when everything is new. But the more time you have, the more you will see.

In areas where there is a good variety of game, you can expect to spend about one-and-a-half hunting days per trophy.

This doesn't take into account specialized hunts such as forest safaris or elephant hunts, but it's a good average that holds up well on plains-game safaris and general-bag safaris. It also doesn't mean that you can take any given animal in that amount of time. In areas where they occur you can probably take common species such as hartebeest, impala, wildebeest, and springbok on any given day, and you might even take two or three varieties on the same day. But you might spend a week or more in the same country before you find the kudu you're looking for.

Of course, even the tough ones like bongo and big elephant can be taken on the first day, but the last day is as good as the first, and the more days you have between the two the better off you are. Quality of area, the experience

Whatever your primary game, there will almost certainly be a number of other species available. These vary from area to area. The blesbok will be found in most South African areas but not elsewhere. Choose the safari based on the primary game, and don't worry too much about what else is (or isn't) on the menu.

Give some thought to your preferences for camp situations. Especially if you're taking non-hunting observers, you may want to shop for a comfortable, well-established permanent camp.

and expertise of your professional hunter, and plain old luck are so important that it is impossible to establish sound rules of thumb on how long it takes to hunt a given animal. Your own skill matters, too. It takes longer if you bungle shots, can't walk, and so on. Also, it depends on how picky you are. While outfitters or governments may enforce minimum lengths of safaris to hunt certain animals, there are no hard-and-fast rules on how long things take. But I can suggest some guidelines based on my experience.

In southern Africa, a plains-game hunt of seven days should yield a kudu and three or four other species; a ten-day hunt should yield six or seven trophies. A buffalo and plains-game hunt is usually ten days, and I think this is about right. Under most circumstances it shouldn't take more than four or five days to get a buffalo, but you will take very little other game while concentrating on buffalo tracks. After you have secured the buffalo, the rest of the hunt should yield four or five additional trophies.

I don't like cat hunts that allow less than two weeks in one area. For lion and leopard there is no such thing as enough hunting days to ensure success, but to give it less than two weeks invites failure. Three weeks is better, but these days most three-week safaris break the hunt into at least two areas. The odds may not be as good on a twenty-one-day hunt in two areas as they are on a fourteen-day hunt in just one area. Remember, the only days that matter are the days spent hunting the cat. Two weeks doesn't ensure success but is enough to do a pretty thorough job of hunting. If the goal is to take both lion and leopard on a single safari (which I have often tried to do but have never accomplished), then three weeks in one area is enough.

Two weeks is plenty of time for Derby eland, but you need three weeks for bongo. It's hard to say how long an elephant hunt should be. To find a hundred-pounder, the three-month safari of the old days would be long enough. But if you're happy to take the first fifty-pounder you encounter, a three-week safari is more than you need. The best rule of thumb is always to book the longest safari you can afford, in terms of both time and money. In the wonderland of African game country, it isn't likely you'll get bored!

ONE-ON-ONE OR TWO-ON-ONE?

People often ask my advice on two hunters sharing a guide. Two hunters sharing a guide can save quite a bit of money, but that doesn't make it a good idea. It largely depends on with whom you share. The second hunter should be someone you know pretty well, and he or she should have similar capabilities as a hunter. It won't work well if one hunter can walk better than the other, and it will work less well if one partner shoots brilliantly while the other misses repeatedly. Under some circumstances, however, two-to-one is a good option that will detract little from each hunter's success. It's OK on almost any plains-game safari or on buffalo. Two-to-one works on a ten-day safari, but it works even better if you add a few days, making it twelve or fourteen days instead of ten. When hunting cats it does not work, with one exception. It's a pretty good deal if two hunters agree that one hunts lion while the other hunts leopard; leopard are best hunted in the evening, while lions are primarily a morning event. But when two hunters both want lion or leopard, forget it. Also, sharing a guide is not appropriate for any of the really difficult prizes.

HOW MUCH SHOULD YOU SPEND?

The cost of African hunting varies widely. There is still a lot of really good plains-game hunting in Namibia, South Africa, and Zimbabwe at a daily rate of about $250 per day. This means that the basic cost of a ten-day safari, for example, is less than the cost of most guided elk hunts in Colorado. As you expand into the Big Five and other prizes, the daily rate usually goes up. This makes sense; outfitters that can offer these trophies have fewer lions to sell than they do buffalo, and fewer buffalo than they have kudu. As you move north from hunting on private land to government concessions, daily rates also tend to escalate, because outfitting costs increase dramatically. Concessions that have dangerous game are astronomically expensive; and the more remote the camp, the more expensive it is to supply.

There aren't any rules of thumb; some countries are more expensive than others, and some outfitters charge more than others. In southern Africa there is very good leopard hunting

The author knows a few people who have started their African hunting with difficult forest hunting, but he doesn't recommend it. It's far better to get your feet wet with a plains-game or buffalo safari in more open country with lots of game.

on private land for $350 to $400 per day, but if you want to hunt your leopard in Zambia or Tanzania, the daily rate will more than double. Buffalo are mostly found on government concessions, and the prices start to go up. Still, good safaris for buffalo and plains game can be found for about $500 to $600 per day. When you get into the classic general-bag safaris that include lion—and also the specialized hunts for elephant and the most prized antelope—you can expect daily rates to run in the neighborhood of $1,000 per day. Some of the top outfitters charge much more. They can do this because of their good reputation and sometimes because they have extraordinarily good areas.

For most of us, budget is the overriding concern when shopping for safaris, so keep this in mind: Quality of area is generally more important than who is hunting it! Some

Tented camps usually aren't as comfortable as lodges or permanent camps, but they're certainly more traditional. If that's what you want, you can find it—but you'll have to make your wishes known.

outfitters are a little better than others in terms of services, and some professional hunters are a little better in terms of skill. But it's unlikely that the very best and highest-priced outfitter is twice as good, or even a third better, than the worst outfitter in a given region. On the other hand, a certain area can be twice as good as another. In other words, it might be worthwhile to pay more to hunt a really good area. But if budget is a concern, it may not be worth the extra cost to hunt with a high-profile outfitter.

Daily rate is just one cost. You must also factor in trophy fees or licenses. These are generally pretty standard within a country, but they add up quickly. If you take a lot of game, the total cost of trophy fees may well exceed the basic safari cost. In the southern African countries there isn't much more to worry about, but in more remote areas you may get nailed with concession fees of some type. In Tanzania you must pay a government tax of $100 per hunting day per person. In Zambia, if you decide to hunt cats, roan, or sable, you have just made the shift from a "mini-safari" to a "classic safari," in their game department's terms, and you will pay a flat fee of $5,000 before you can buy the licenses. You may only be able to reach your hunting area by an air charter, and if significant distances are involved, air charters can be frightfully expensive. It's pretty easy to figure the daily rate, then add in the trophy fees and come up with a basic safari cost—but you should always ask "what else" and get it in writing.

"What else" will include preparation and shipping of trophies, tips, and hotel costs before and after the safari. We'll talk about these in later chapters. I have to say that I have never run into a genuine "hidden cost" on any African hunt. But sometimes the matrix of daily rate, trophy fees, concession fees, charter fees, and extras is complex, and it takes a bit of work to come up with a genuine bottom line. Before you compare, you must have the bottom line.

ANYTHING ELSE?

Non-hunting observers are welcome in most camps, and, unless expensive air charters are involved, the costs are usually minimal. However, the more remote and more specialized a safari, the less fun it is for someone who isn't actually participating in the hunt. African camps are uniformly wonderful; even in the remotest areas the level of service is better than anywhere else in the world. But in such areas there isn't much besides the camp, and on a typical elephant or bongo hunt your companion will not have much other game to view. Most safaris are wonderful to share with your significant other,

Game ranches in extreme southern Africa have a wealth of wildlife and truly fabulous hunting, but you must understand that game fences have become a way of life. If this bothers you, and it bothers many, then you need to hunt farther north.

whether he or she hunts or not; some safaris are not. Ask your outfitter. Before speaking with outfitters, you need to establish in your own mind a clear picture of what you expect. Then you must be able to articulate your expectations as you shop for your safari. Professional hunters are not only in the hunting business but in the entertainment business, and the really successful ones figured this out a long time ago.

It's no different from hunting in North America: If you want to hunt from a comfortable lodge, you don't book a backpack hunt. In Africa, if you want a tented camp in a remote wilderness, you should book that kind of safari. You'll be well fed and well cared for, but don't expect the same kind of amenities you would find in a hunting lodge in South Africa. There's a sad, but absolutely true, story about a Central African professional hunter who was served

When deciding to go on a safari, do not forget the spouse and kids. It is a great experience for them, too. This young hunter shot his first zebra at age 9. (Photo: Safari Press library)

with a lawsuit when he visited the States. The plaintiff's primary complaint was that the PH failed to have diet soft drinks in camp!

If you have any physical limitations, you must be forthcoming about them. Much African hunting is available to people with even severe limitations, but if there are medical considerations or if walking is a problem, you need to be honest up front. An honest outfitter won't take a booking that he knows will be a failure; his continued success depends upon your success. Some situations are less arduous than others, depending on what you intend to hunt and also on road access and trafficability. This is all common-sense stuff—but you need to use all of that precious commodity you have available. Shopping for a safari is a confusing process. The options are endless, and every professional hunter in Africa, as well as his agents, would like to take your booking. It's easier for everybody if you decide, early on, what you want and what you can afford. In the next chapter we'll turn to the mechanics of actually booking a safari.

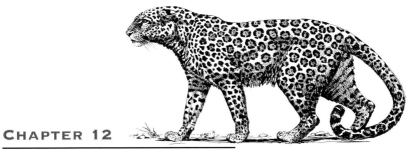

CHAPTER 12

HOW TO BOOK A SAFARI

There's no mystery and little intrigue—just remember the five Ps: Prior planning prevents poor performance!

It is relatively difficult to have a bad hunt in Africa. Sure, there are a few unscrupulous outfitters, but they are easy to weed out. Sure, it is possible for a good outfitter to go bad or turn in a bad performance: Outfitters are people; people have problems; and problems, whether personal or related to business or health, can result in bad safaris. This, too, is relatively rare in Africa, in part because a professional hunter's license is difficult to obtain in most African countries today. Those who have one don't want to lose it. The other, and perhaps most important, factor is that Africa truly is a hunter's paradise, even at the beginning of the new millennium.

Most African hunting areas offer a wide variety of game. There is much to see and much hunting to be done. Provided you have taken reasonable care in selecting your outfitter, I simply can't imagine a "bad" safari. I can imagine an unsuccessful safari—one that fails to result in the taking of the primary game sought. I have been on unsuccessful safaris for lion, leopard, elephant, buffalo, kudu, sitatunga, giant eland, and bongo—and that isn't a complete list. None of these safaris were bad. Some of them rate among my most memorable hunts. In most cases I saw the primary game, but it was not of the quality desired, and I took other species of game. That's hunting; there are no guarantees.

In most cases your decision about where to hunt will be based on the game that is most important to you. Many first-timers want buffalo as part of the bag, and there are several good options. This bull was taken in Zambia, a great buffalo area.

African hunting, even for the difficult prizes, tends to be successful—far more successful than much North American hunting. One reason is that there is lots of game. Also, most African professional hunters are just that: experienced professional hunters who know their business and are backed up by a staff of experienced trackers and skinners who are just as professional in their own right. Another important factor is that weather is rarely a problem. Yes, late rains can cause difficulties well into the dry season, and either too much or too little rain can alter game movement. Unexpected poaching or local hunting pressure occurs only once in a while.

In African hunting there are imponderables that no outfitter can plan for. But in North America entire hunts can get rained out, snowed out, or blown out by high winds. This does not happen during the primary hunting months

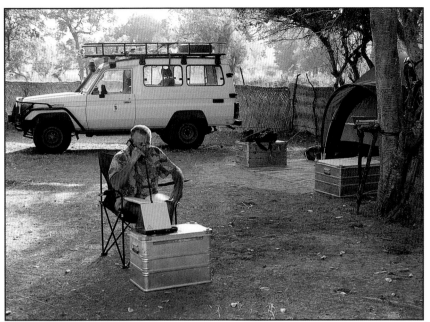

Alain Lefol in his "office" in southern Chad. Satellite phones make direct communication with Africa much easier than ever before, but you still can't expect a PH in the field to have time to answer all the questions that may arise.

in Africa, meaning July through September in most areas of southern Africa. June is also OK, but the grass may be high, depending on the rains. October can be very good but is extremely hot in some areas. In the north, above the equator, the best and driest months reverse to December through March, but bongo hunting is best after the rains begin, meaning late April through June or July. It is quite practical to hunt throughout the year in a few countries, such as Namibia and Ethiopia. Sometimes you can get a "deal" by booking a hunt during an odd time of year. How wise this is depends partly on what you're hunting, but mostly on how much rain there is in that particular year. In other words, you're betting on luck.

Luck is a factor in all hunting. To a degree you make your own luck by putting yourself in the right area at the right time, then doing the right things when your chance comes along. But even if you and your PH do all the right things, you still may not get a chance at the game you want most. The relative difficulty of the quarry you seek, how much time you have, and how picky you are can influence the outcome. I have a friend who is an extremely selective hunter. He does his homework, hunts hard, and shoots well—but he wants only the best. If he doesn't find an animal that meets his trophy criteria, he's perfectly happy to come home empty-handed. This is the right attitude, but since his standards are very high, he isn't always successful. I'm just the opposite. I like big trophies just as much as anybody else, but I'm more interested in a good hunt—and, business being business, something I can write about. So I take a few very good trophies mixed in with average specimens. My overall success is quite high, not because I'm a better hunter than my friend, but because my personal standards are lower. Keep this in mind. You will not encounter record-book animals—let alone the "top ten"—of every variety. Your PH should be able to offer general guidelines on what his area is likely to produce. The more reasonable your expectations, the more successful you will be.

By now you should have a pretty good idea what animals you wish to hunt. As we've seen, the "what" may drive the "where." The "when" may be driven by specific seasons in a given country, or by the best times for certain animals in certain places. No matter how it shakes out, you will almost certainly have some hard choices to make among different countries, areas within countries, and the potential outfitters, which can number in the dozens.

When you study the magazine ads and walk the aisles at hunters' conventions, the most prevalent marketers of safaris will be the outfitters. Some are so well known that they have achieved near-celebrity status; others keep a lower profile, and there are always new faces. There is nothing wrong, and everything right, with booking a known outfitter who has a proven track record. On the other hand, a lesser-known or newer outfitter may charge considerably less for almost identical services. The risks may seem greater, but keep in mind that a newer, younger organization is anxious to develop a reputation and may work hard to accomplish that. Also— and this is very important—under most circumstances it is

Professional hunter Rudy Lubin in camp in the C.A.R. One of the problems is that good PHs are without communications for months at a time, so it isn't always easy to locate them and secure a booking.

extremely unlikely that you will actually hunt with the outfitter himself.

Most hunting companies have a handful of professional hunters in their employ. The outfitter is probably also a professional hunter, but if he's one of the famous names, he is likely to book himself up with repeat clients long before you get to him. This means that your safari will be assigned to one of the other PHs, and this is the person upon whose shoulders rests your success. The outfitter is important—he is the guy who provides the hunting areas and the logistics— but don't book your hunt on the strength of his personality, because he probably won't be in camp with you. Now, you can demand that you hunt with the outfitter as a condition of booking. If it's really important to you that you hunt with this guy personally, that's exactly what you should do. But this is not always the best course.

The outfitter is the boss, and in a large company he may have numerous boss-type details to take care of. If there are logistical problems, he has to solve them. If one of his PHs gets sick or hurt, he has to find a replacement. If one of his PHs is having trouble with a difficult client (or vice versa), he has to sort it out. Much of this can be done via radio and satellite phone, so it may not interfere with your hunt—but it can. A professional hunter who is not also the outfitter has you as his primary responsibility; the outfitter has responsibility for the whole outfit. For this reason many outfitters do not personally guide safaris—and some that do should not. So don't ever think that the only way to get a good hunt is to hunt personally with the boss. If he's a good outfitter, he also has good PHs working for him, and you have to trust that to the outfit's overall reputation.

Longtime booking agent Jack Atcheson Sr. has been one of my mentors in this business for nearly thirty years now.

He once offered the following bit of advice on booking a
hunt. At that particular moment we were talking primarily
about North American hunting, but I think this applies
equally well in Africa. Jack told me to "always consider the
area first." Concessions change hands, but it's the quality
of the area that is most important in determining the
quantity and quality of game you will encounter. If you
want sable, you must go to an area that has sable. If you
want big sable, you must go to an area that produces big
sable—and there are very, very few areas that do. If you
want lion, you should go to the best lion area you can find,
and again there are few. Especially if you have extremely

*A much younger Boddington and a young Russ Broom with a couple of very
good Zambian buffalo. Back then Russ was a beginning hunter, making up
for experience with energy and enthusiasm. An enthusiastic youngster can give
you a great hunt . . . but not necessarily better than an experienced old hand.*

specific desires for certain game, your choice of area should take priority over a certain outfitter.

It is not easy to determine the best area for the game you desire. The *SCI All-time Record Book of Trophy Animals* (which we will call the SCI record book) is one of the best tools, but you must be careful in its use. Most of the animals listed therein were taken fairly recently, but things change so rapidly in Africa that information just a decade old may not be useful. In researching good areas for certain animals, the best course is to obtain the most recent edition of the SCI record book and scan the listings for animals taken within the last five or six years. *Safari* magazine is also an invaluable resource for current information. Read not only the hunt reports but also the stories.

After the area, you should next consider the professional hunter—not the outfitter but the actual PH who will lead your safari. This requires even more research. The outfitter probably has the best-known name, but, as we've seen, you may not hunt with him personally. Quite honestly, I have a great deal of faith in African professional hunters, so I have never specified a certain PH when arranging a hunt. But, then, I've got a lot of experience, and it doesn't bother me if I hunt with an unknown youngster. If this is your first safari, I recommend you hunt with a well-seasoned PH. And then there are special situations that require special skills. If you're going elephant hunting, you are best served by hunting with a PH who has a lot of experience with elephant. Cat hunting is different; relatively few PHs are really good at hunting lion and/or leopard. If you want to hunt the cats, you need to find one of these few PHs. The same holds true for hunting bongo and any of the other difficult species. The same resources— record books, hunt reports, magazine stories—should yield names of professional hunters. However, there is no substitute for word of mouth.

This is hard to come by. Relatively few of us know a lot of people who have hunted Africa recently, especially at the beginning of our African experience. If you are contemplating a safari, I strongly recommend that you choke it up and spend the few hundred bucks required to attend the annual Safari Club Convention. It is the largest gathering of international hunters in the world. There you can meet and talk to people who have hunted the areas and animals you are interested in, and you can speak with the outfitters and PHs you are considering. You can also meet a tremendous number of professional hunters personally. This face-to-face contact is not mandatory, but it's the very best way to get answers to questions and, above all, to ensure that you will be hunting with someone you like. (By the way, this works both ways!)

It is not always possible to separate the professional hunter from the outfitter—or the outfitter from the area—but, at least theoretically, I think choosing the outfitter is the third priority. Outfitters are usually better represented than PHs at the conventions, so you will be able to meet them as well. But whether we're talking outfitters or professional hunters, or both, always check references. Ask for recent references, no older than the last couple of seasons, and call them. You will get a better response over the phone than by writing them. Be reasonable about the time of day you call and how long you keep them on the phone, but don't feel bad about calling references. Nobody I know is busier than I am, but if I'm on a PH's reference list it is because I like that PH, and I know I'm doing him a service by taking a referral call. E-mail is also a good means of communication, but remember that in all written communication the information you get back is only as good as the questions you ask.

Keep in mind that few outfitters will supply unfavorable references, so give some thought to the questions you will ask.

End-of-hunt paperwork at the conclusion of a Tanzanian safari. There will always be last-minute accounting and details to take care of, but you have to decide whether to handle the paperwork yourself or have an agent smooth the way for you.

Ask the references about the specific areas they hunted, the time of year they hunted, the game they spotted as well as the game they took, and the results of any other safaris with the same outfit of which they might be aware. When talking to any reference, always ask how many times he or she has been to Africa. This is important, because it's part of the African syndrome that we all become instant experts on the last day of our first safari. It happened to me and it will happen to you, so don't be sensitive about it—just take it as a given. At the conclusion of that marvelous, never-to-be-equaled experience, the new expert is almost certain to believe that the professional hunter who led that first African safari is larger-than-life, an amalgamation of Tarzan, Philip Percival, and Karamojo Bell. Don't discount the information and the recommendation, but take experience into account. By the way, you are always within your rights to ask to see a current professional hunter's license,

Joe Bishop, Alain Lefol, and Jean-Christophe Lefol combine GPS (Global Positioning System) and map as they search for likely places to find bongo. When things get tough it takes a lot of experience to know what to do next.

valid for the country you will be hunting. And it's a good idea to stick with people who belong to their local professional hunters' organization and the International Professional Hunters Association (IPHA).

Should you book direct or go through a booking agent? Some hunters have strong feelings about this and prefer never to go through an agent. I'm just the opposite. I believe strongly in going through a reputable booking agent. It should cost no more. There are outfitters who give a discount for booking directly, and I guess that's their right, but I'm always a bit suspicious of this practice—especially if they use agents some of the time. Other outfitters refuse to use agents; however, I like to use them. I don't need to use one: I know most of the players in the business, I know how to book airline flights, I know how to get visas, I know what shots to take, I know what gear to pack, and so forth. I just find it a whole lot easier, simpler, and more convenient to let an expert help with these myriad details.

This is equally true of arranging hunts at conventions. Once the convention is over, the PH goes back to Africa. Communication is difficult at best, and it can be impossible after the season gets started. A booking agent can answer questions as they arise and can keep you posted on how the hunting is going with a given outfitter or area in the months (and sometimes years) prior to your safari. From the standpoint of practicality, the agent also stands available to help if problems arise and to mediate if, God forbid, something should go wrong. The way to do this at a convention is simply to ask the outfitter if he has an agent he would like you to go through. Or, if you've been talking to an agent and have developed confidence in him or her, ask the PH if you can arrange the hunt through that company. There are few genuine exclusives, and most PHs and outfitters are delighted to have someone else handle the paperwork.

How far ahead you should book depends on the situation. Hunting is a supply-and-demand business, just like everything else. A given outfit has a certain number of safaris to sell during a hunting season of known length; once they're booked up, that's the end of it unless there's a cancellation. If your research has suggested that a certain window of time is much better for the game you wish to hunt, then you should plan on booking at least a full year ahead, sometimes two years. Ditto if you want to hunt with a certain PH. If exact safari dates and personalities aren't critical, then it is usually possible to get a booking by early January of the year you intend to hunt. The hunting conventions usually start in mid-January, and during this period the remaining good dates with the better outfitters usually go quickly.

Deposit amounts, payment schedules, and cancellation policies vary widely among outfitters and agents. Most outfitters and agents are pretty good about working with people when genuine problems crop up, but, properly, your deposit is your word that you will be there—and the outfitter's livelihood depends on it. The later in the game you change your mind, the less likely you are to receive a refund. That's if you cancel.

Africa is an uncertain place. Political problems are always possible, and entire countries have closed with no notice. Outfitters can also go out of business or run into catastrophic problems that leave booked clients hanging. Properly, the outfitter should refund your deposit under such circumstances. Practically speaking, this won't always happen. Deposit money is often used to purchase equipment, lease concessions, and promote the business, and it simply may not exist to be

Ronnie MacFarlane tending to some normal business. Even the best outfitters will have punctures and get their vehicles stuck. The issue isn't how often but whether they have the equipment and know-how to handle the problem quickly and continue the hunt.

returned to you. I tend to believe that deposit money is safest with a good agent, who will hold it in an escrow account until he must forward it to Africa. Should you need to cancel, an agent is usually better able than either you or the outfitter to find a replacement hunter. Trip insurance is inexpensive and covers all the bases. The little details are not many, but they will get you.

If you haven't made plans in advance, there are often last-minute cancellations that offer considerable savings. I usually don't have much flexibility, so I've let some great deals slip away. However, the problem with last-minute safaris is that the details can become very difficult. International flights to and from Africa are limited. Schedules probably won't be available at the time you book your safari, but you should work on airline reservations six months ahead, and by no means less than three months ahead. If you're using a booking agent, he or she may also have a travel agency; or the booking agent can recommend an "African-literate" travel agent. If you make the airline reservations yourself, make sure you use an agent who has experience booking African travel.

Visa requirements vary from country to country, and the requirements change. Always ask your outfitter and/or agent if a visa is required. If so, I strongly recommend using a professional visa service, and get the ball rolling no later than six weeks prior to your safari, especially if you have other travel that requires you to use a passport.

Right now about half of the common hunting destinations require gun permits up front. Your outfitter should provide the forms. Get them done well ahead; make absolutely certain the serial numbers are accurate; and don't change anything. Make sure the rifles you put on your permit are available and serviceable, and once you have submitted that form, don't change your mind. Murphy being the optimist he is, there is little chance that a last-minute

Time of year can be just as important as the area, and the best time may be different for different species. The Selous Game Reserve, for instance, is one of the best places for huge eland, but they're very difficult to hunt until late in the season.

A convention is a good place to meet African outfitters. This is the Dallas Safari Club gathering, where the people are known for their hospitality. (Photo: Safari Press library)

When booking a two on one safari keep in mind that even a small animal like this red-flanked duiker may be on limited license and only one hunter will be able to shoot one. (Photo: Safari Press library)

change will be properly acted upon by all parties. Also, make sure the amount of ammunition on the form matches the amount you take with you.

Relatively few inoculations are required for entry into African countries, but some of them—like the inoculation for yellow fever—are not readily available from your country doctor in rural America. The Red Cross publishes a list of the required and recommended inoculations. This is another chore to take care of at least a month before departure. Malaria is endemic in most parts of interior Africa. During the dry season the actual risk of exposure is limited, but the prophylaxis does work, so it's foolish not to take it.

Relatively few African trophies require CITES import permits from the U.S. Fish and Wildlife Service. Leopard, bontebok, white rhino, and elephant are among those that do. Some African countries require you to have the CITES permit before the hunt; others do not. But the permit costs just $25, and it's best to have it in hand.

There is no free lunch. Inoculations, visas, airline tickets, gun permits, and hotels and meals while traveling all add to the cost of your safari. So does dipping, packing, and shipping of your trophies. Budgets are important for most of us, so at some point, early on, you need to get a fairly accurate accounting of what these things will cost. If you're using a booking agency, they should be able to provide this information. Your outfitter should be able to give accurate figures on everything on his end, but he may not have a clue about the assorted little details. Most outfitters are good about spelling out daily rates, license and trophy fees, and such, but I have found many to be a bit vague about costs beyond their direct control, such as air charters and trophy shipment. You may have to press hard to get these details, but you must get them before you commit. Air charters in Africa can be frightfully expensive and can radically alter the cost comparison of one outfit to another.

Generally speaking, however, there are few surprises, and most outfitters within a certain country will be priced within a narrow range. As usual, if something seems too good to be true, it probably is. You may have to pay extra for a high-profile outfitter's reputation, and he may be well worth it. But make sure he has good areas to back up his reputation.

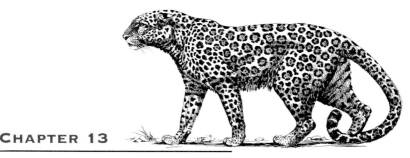

CHAPTER 13

GUNS AND GEAR

With equipment, pack light; with rifles, think "versatile."

An African safari is a grand adventure. When most of us first journey to the Dark Continent, it is the most exotic, most remote, most distant hunting locale in our experience. We worry endlessly about making sure we have all the right gear and the perfect guns and loads. This is harmless and quite healthy. Laying out the gear and packing and repacking the gun case and duffel bags is an important part of any pre-hunt ritual, and it adds to the anticipation. The paradox is that properly packing for an African hunt is one of the easiest things you can do.

Africa is one of the least gear-intensive places to hunt in the entire world. You don't have to worry about cold-weather gear, hip waders, sleeping bags, camping equipment, or load-carrying devices for packing meat and trophies. Your clothes really will be washed every day or so, so you don't need more than a couple of changes. Packing for Africa is simple, but you do want to take the "right stuff."

GUNS

Volumes have been written about rifles and cartridges for African hunting, and indeed I wrote one of them. The sheer variety of African game is daunting, and choosing exactly the right rifles and cartridges is a fascinating study. However, the tendency is to make the simple altogether too complex. African

The key word in African rifles for anything other than dangerous game is versatility. You never know what you might encounter, and you will use the same rifle for everything from tiny antelope to eight-hundred-pound zebra.

It's difficult to imagine a rifle as useful for African hunting as a scoped .375 H&H. This is a new Winchester Model 70 Classic, with controlled-round feed and good iron sights, mounted with a Leupold 1.5–5X—truly an African classic.

game ranges in size from the tiny dik-dik up to the elephant. Undoubtedly there is a "perfect" rifle and cartridge for every variety of game and every type of terrain. However, it is impossible to take to Africa the perfect combination for all of the game you are likely to encounter on a given safari. You must compromise, and this means versatility is extremely important.

The traditional African battery is based on a "light rifle" for most of the antelope; a "medium rifle" for the larger antelope and perhaps lion; and a "heavy rifle" for the thick-skinned game. The concept remains valid in theory. For example, if you're a "gun guy" and you are planning a true general-bag safari of twenty-one days or more, which will include the full mix of game from smallest to largest, then the old three-rifle battery remains sound. For most modern safaris, however, three rifles are at least one too many. Today's safaris are shorter, bag limits are far more restricted, and in some cases (Zambia being a good example) you may be legally restricted to just two rifles on a gun permit.

There is some validity to the old saw, "Two's company, three's a crowd." Under most circumstances you can conveniently take two rifles in the hunting vehicle. When you leave the truck to take a walk, follow tracks, or make a stalk, you will probably carry the rifle you think you are most likely to use, but it isn't a problem to have a tracker carry the second rifle "just in case." With three rifles the choice becomes confusing—and you will find that one of the three spends most of its time cased in camp. So think about a maximum of two rifles.

With two rifles, versatility becomes even more important, but there's not a lot of mystery involved. Rather than "light, medium, and heavy," it's easier to think of a two-rifle battery in terms of "lighter and heavier." The lighter of the two will probably see more use. You will use it for camp meat, bait animals, and plains-game trophies ranging from small antelope to fairly stout beasts such as wildebeest, zebra, perhaps sable, and kudu. This means that your lighter rifle may take animals

This is a pair of Rigby rifles the author had built for thornbush hunting. The bottom rifle is the old .350 Rigby Rimless Magnum; the top, a .416 Rigby. Together they will do anything, provided the ranges are kept to about 250 yards, preferably much closer.

as small as a big jack rabbit and as large and tough as a bull elk. You will use the heavier rifle much less, but it's very important because you will use it to hunt any thick-skinned dangerous game that is on the menu. You may also use it to hunt lion and the largest plains game, such as moose-sized eland.

You will use the light rifle almost every day, and you may use it to take shots that range from very close to several hundred yards away. Properly, it should be a rifle that you are very familiar and comfortable with. However, if we're limiting our battery to just two rifles, it's best to choose the heavier of the two first, because the nature of your bigger rifle can limit the sensible selection of your lighter caliber.

Obviously, the genuine need for a big-bore depends altogether on whether or not you will be hunting dangerous game. But let's assume that your safari will include buffalo at a minimum. It's obvious that you need a rifle that's adequate

On several occasions the author has carried only his pet 8mm Remington Magnum. It's a good choice only for specialized hunting, where ranges might be long and there is no dangerous game. It was perfect for mountain nyala in Ethiopia.

for the task, and just as obvious that the rifle you choose for impala, reedbuck, and waterbuck probably isn't. You need to make a fundamental choice between a true big-bore, probably a bolt-action .458 or a double rifle of .450 or larger, and a "large medium," probably a .375 or a .416. For buffalo there are no wrong choices in this spectrum.

The .375 H&H should be considered the sensible minimum for buffalo; it was adequate in 1912 and it remains adequate today. The .416s will achieve quicker and more dramatic results with identical shot placement. The genuine big-bores from .450 upward are more impressive yet. If you have a big double or a heavy bolt-action—or have a burning desire to acquire one—there is no reason not to. You will be properly armed for buffalo, and this is exactly what you should have if you will be hunting elephant. The .375, although hardly overpowering for buffalo, will do the job. It is marginal for elephant, especially in the thick cover where they are hunted today. The .416s, to my mind, are perfect for buffalo and also not overpowering for elephant.

For any of the really big game, from Cape buffalo upward, it is correct to choose one of the true big-bores. The difficulty is that the .375s and .416s are versatile rifles. They are powerful enough for the big stuff but flat shooting enough to handle the larger plains game. Most .375s and .416s will be scoped, adding greatly to their utility. If your heavier rifle is a scoped .375 or .416, then you have a perfect rifle for lion and eland, and also a rifle that you can use for larger plains game such as zebra and kudu and perhaps sable and roan. A true big-bore, caliber .450 and upward, is not versatile. Nothing is more effective on the largest of game, but that is all the big-bores are for. Period. Even if the rifle is scoped, most of the large calibers are too slow and their trajectory is too arcing for sensible use on plains game.

So if you decide you want your heavier rifle to be a true big-bore, your second rifle must be suitable for everything else you intend to hunt. This means that a .30 magnum is probably the minimum caliber to pair with a big-bore. A .33 or a .35 is probably better yet, and if you plan to hunt lion and/or eland, your second rifle may need to be a .375. There's nothing wrong with any of this; just keep in mind that a true big-bore is a short-ranged, specialized affair, so the second rifle of your battery must be very versatile. It will be the rifle you use most of the time. In fact, if your safari includes just one buffalo license, then you probably will use your big-bore only on that one buffalo. The second, lighter rifle will do everything else.

If, on the other hand, you opt for a scoped .375 or .416 as your heavier rifle, then your second rifle can take the form of your favorite deer rifle, perhaps a .270, a 7mm, or any .30-caliber. You will probably use the heavier rifle on a couple of the larger antelopes as well as on the dangerous game. The lighter rifle will be used even more.

A one-rifle battery is an option. In the forest, where shots will be close and trouble with elephant is always possible, I have taken only a .416 and have been perfectly happy. In places such as Namibia and Ethiopia, where shots can be long and I won't be hunting any dangerous game, I've taken only a .340 Weatherby or an 8mm Remington Magnum (my pet) and have been perfectly happy. Under most circumstances, however, a .375 is the only sensible choice for a one-rifle battery, especially if you plan to hunt dangerous game. The reason is that not only is caliber .375 the traditional minimum for the bad boys, but it is also the legal minimum in numerous African countries. It should be said that the old .375 H&H, as wonderful as it is, is not the only .375-caliber cartridge. Others in that bore diameter include .375 Dakota, .375 Remington Ultra Mag,

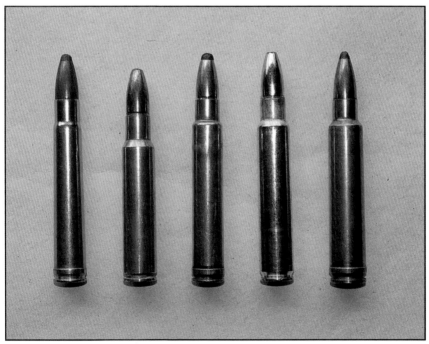

(left to right) .375 H&H Magnum, .375 Dakota Magnum, .375 Weatherby Magnum, .375 Remington Ultra Mag, .378 Weatherby Magnum. When you think .375, the good old H&H is no longer the only option. The faster .375s extend the effective range, but the price is considerably more recoil.

215

.375 Weatherby Magnum, and the behemoth .378 Weatherby Magnum. Listed more or less in ascending order of velocity, all are faster than the .375 H&H and thus shoot flatter. But, also in ascending order, all produce more recoil.

Depending on your personal interests, centerfire rifles may not comprise the only arms choices you need to make. Most African hunting areas offer bird shooting that varies from good to fabulous. Most outfits keep a shotgun in camp, but don't expect a double Purdey or a nice Browning. The professional hunter's shotgun is usually a multi-purpose tool, used primarily for following up leopard, dispatching snakes that slither into camp, and hunting small duiker. Because of the general scarcity of shot shells, bird shooting is usually pretty far down on the list of priorities, and the "camp shotgun" is probably a short-barreled and well-battered pump gun.

If you're a keen bird shooter, take your own shotgun. Shot shells do count against the five-kilogram (11 pounds) ammunition limit imposed by the airlines. You may have room to slip in a couple of boxes of high-base No. 6 shot shells, which will do for a couple of afternoons of guinea fowl and francolin shooting—but if you're serious, make sure your outfitter lays in a supply of shot shells for you. If you aren't a serious wingshooter but would like to sample some bird shooting, find out if there will be a shotgun in camp, and bring along a couple of boxes of shells. Twelve-gauge is almost universal in Africa, but do make sure it's legal to bring ammunition without a matching firearm; and if there's a gun permit, put the shot shells on the permit.

Very few African countries have restrictions against muzzleloaders, but only a few allow handguns. Those that allow them, at this writing, include South Africa, Zimbabwe, Namibia, Tanzania, and C.A.R.—but this is subject to change. This is one of the specific questions that you must ask your outfitter and/or agent at the time of booking. Exactly the same can be said of archery tackle. Slowly, slowly, thanks largely to Safari

Club International's avid bow hunters, Africa is opening up to bowhunting—but if you plan on using anything other than a centerfire rifle, you must ask the question before you plunk down your deposit. With bowhunting the situation is not much different from the way it is in North America; some outfitters have experience with bow hunters and are set up for their different hunting techniques, but many are not.

AMMUNITION

The primary considerations are what kind of ammunition and how much. Because of the great variety of African game, your choice of bullet is important—and the bullet you choose must be tough enough for the largest animal you plan to hunt. Theoretically, it is possible to take a quick-expanding softpoint for impala-sized game and a tougher, controlled-expansion design for the bigger stuff, but in practice I find this far too confusing. It is better to select just one softpoint that is tough enough for anything you might run into. To me, this means that Africa is the place for the very best hunting bullets. Nosler Partitions are a good baseline and are never a bad choice, but, depending on what your rifle shoots the best, other good African bullets include Barnes X, Winchester Fail Safe, Trophy Bonded Bear Claw, and Swift A-Frame. Stick with bullets that are relatively heavy for caliber, and you can't go too far wrong.

I believe in a good softpoint for the first shot on buffalo, but you will want a few solids for backup—and you will want solids only for elephant, hippo, and rhino. I'm not aware of any "bad" solids currently on the market, but I have had excellent results with Hornady and Woodleigh steel-jacketed solids, and with homogenous alloy solids from Barnes and A-Square. Other excellent designs include Speer's tungsten-core, full-metal-jacket bullet and the Trophy Bonded Sledgehammer solid.

(left to right) 7mm Remington Magnum, .30-06, .300 Winchester Magnum. For general plains-game hunting, your favorite deer rifle is probably hard to beat. The author has had excellent results with the .30-06, but the 7mm and .30 magnum rifles are also great.

The amount of game you will hunt dictates the amount of ammunition you will need, but the overarching limit is the airlines' five-kilogram rule. On a lengthy modern safari, sixty rounds for the lighter rifle and thirty rounds for the heavier rifle should be plenty. If you do not plan to hunt elephant with the larger caliber, you should take twenty softpoints and ten solids. If you're hunting elephant, I'd go half-and-half. If your two rifles are a .375 or a .416 plus a lighter rifle, then forty rounds for each rifle should be adequate. If you have doubts, figure an average of two rounds for each animal you intend to shoot. (Chances are you will have many one-shot kills, but some animals will take more than one shot, and you might miss occasionally.) Then add in a cushion of ten to twenty rounds for initial sight-in and periodic checking of your sights. Make sure you weigh your ammunition before adding in shot shells. The best way to fit in shotgun ammo is to take just one rifle with fifty rounds. Even then, if you're a serious

Much is made of caliber selection, but bullet selection is equally important. African bullets need to be tough because of the range of game encountered. These are Nosler Partitions, Winchester Fail Safes, and Barnes X-Bullet. Other good choices include the Swift A-Frame and the Trophy Bonded Bear Claw.

bird shooter, there is no way you can take enough shot shells for Africa, so you must coordinate with your outfitter to make sure he has shells of the right gauge in camp.

OPTICS

You want the best optics you can afford, but that doesn't mean the most powerful. There is very little genuine long-range shooting in Africa. On a flat-shooting, versatile rifle to be used on a wide range of plains game, there is no need for a scope of higher magnification than the popular 3–9X or 3.5–10X variables. On a more powerful rifle that might be used on dangerous game and that probably will not be used much past two hundred yards, I like the low-range variables of 1.75–5X or 1.5–6X. Actually, however, a simple fixed 4X will do just fine almost anywhere in Africa and on almost any African hunting rifle. One important consideration: Especially on powerful, hard-kicking rifles, make absolutely certain your scope has enough eye relief. Many scopes that are optically wonderful, including some of the very best brands, simply do not have enough eye relief. Africa is not the place to get cut eyebrows and the resultant flinch.

With the possible exception of the forest, you will use your binoculars a great deal in Africa, day in and day out. I recommend good-quality, full-size binoculars in the 7X42 to 10X40 range, the former in thornbush and the latter in plains, deserts, or mountains. You do not need the added light-gathering capability of larger objective lenses, as in 7X50 or 8X56, so there is no reason to carry the added bulk and weight. Normally I do not take a spotting scope, but there are exceptions, such as when hunting mountain nyala in Ethiopia or Barbary sheep in Chad. In thornbush areas the shooting ranges aren't so great that a range finder is really necessary, but the same exceptions apply, including any plains or desert areas where longer shots are likely.

Cameras are important to me, but this varies with the individual. Even if you don't care a whit about getting nice wildlife and scenic photography, you should care about getting some good trophy shots. Whatever format you like to use, I recommend no less than two cameras (I often carry four), and if you really want a picture of something, you should snap it with two cameras, just to make sure. I figure one-and-a-half to two rolls of film per hunting day, and don't forget extra batteries that fit any device requiring batteries, from cameras to range finders to lighted scope reticles.

CLOTHING

Here's where packing for Africa starts to get simple. On most safaris two sets of hunting clothes are perfectly adequate. If you know you're going to be moving around a lot, such as traveling to several different ranches in South Africa, make it three sets. Do the same if you're on a rainy season bongo or elephant hunt, because drying laundry takes extra time. Camouflage remains illegal in some southern countries, and because of this I stay away from it. Traditional khaki is really too bright in most thornbush and in all forest areas, but a nondescript olive green is good almost everywhere. I prefer to wear shorts and short-sleeved shirts most of the time, because it's not only cooler but quieter. However, you will get cut more by thorns and you will need more sunscreen, so take your choice. If you go with shorts, be advised that you'll need "longs" as well, because in many areas it is much too cold for shorts in the early morning. I also do not wear shorts in the

Good binoculars are important. Magnification of 7X or 8X is about right in thornbush country; 10X is better in more open areas. The author always carries a full-size 35mm camera, but he also carries a smaller "point and shoot" for backup.

forest. Even though it's plenty warm, the exposure to biting ants and other bugs is just too much. In the forest I wear long trousers and long sleeves, and I use military "blousing bands" (stout rubber bands also work) around my ankles, turning the pants cuffs inside them to keep out crawly things. This is also good protection against ticks in bad tick areas, such as coastal South Africa.

With the exception of the few genuine mountain hunts, you don't need serious hiking books in Africa, and in fact they're a detriment because they're too noisy. For the last several years I've worn Russell's "Professional Hunter" boots, ankle-high with canvas panels. High-top tennis shoes also work extremely well. In footwear three things are important: that it be well broken in and comfortable, be able to dry quickly, and have soles that are soft enough to be quiet. Most African professional hunters recommend against wearing socks because they pick up sharp

On left are Rocky safari boots; on right, Russell PH boots—both pairs well used. Some African hunting requires a lot of walking, so boots must be well broken in. Canvas or leather is fine, but make sure the soles are soft and quiet.

bits of grass. That's true enough, but my feet are accustomed to wearing socks and I get blisters when I don't wear them. So I wear socks and pick the stems out of them when I have to. Roll your own on that, but always take care of your feet!

OUTERWEAR

I cannot stress enough how cold it can be in the mornings and sometimes in the evenings, especially when traveling in the dark in an open vehicle. It is possible to get snowed on in South Africa's mountains, and temperatures below freezing are quite possible during the African winter (June through July) in southern Africa and in both Masailand and Ethiopia's high country, due to the elevation. Warm clothes aren't essential in Central Africa but are absolutely mandatory in most other areas. I usually wear a wool sweater and a wind-breaking parka with a watch cap or hood and gloves. The days tend to warm up very quickly once the sun comes up, but early mornings can be brutal. Rain is unlikely during the dry season and almost a sure thing during the rainy season. Either way, I always carry a lightweight rain suit just in case. I have never been bothered a great deal by bugs, but for sitting in leopard blinds or sitatunga machans a "shoo-bug" jacket is a godsend.

For headgear I usually wear a broad-brimmed hat, but that is primarily because I'm sun-sensitive. In truth, a broad-brimmed hat is a pain in thornbush and tends to blow off when traveling in an open vehicle. A baseball cap makes a lot more sense, and I usually trade off between the two.

OTHER GEAR

There ain't much! A minimal amount of gun-cleaning gear—takedown rod, oil, some patching material—is a good idea. Daily gun care is essential during rainy-season hunts, and dust and dirt will build up quickly in the dry season. You should take good sunglasses and sunscreen, and some strong insect repellent. Anything with a lot of DEET works well on most African bugs; nothing works particularly well on tsetse flies. Obviously, you also want to pack any and all medications and toilet articles for the full duration of your safari, and "town clothes" for traveling and any sightseeing you intend to do before and after.

Your professional hunter and your booking agent probably have good "gear lists" in their literature. Everyone has slightly different tastes and requirements, and you should take whatever you need to feel comfortable and be comfortable—but you can pack very light for most safaris. Overpacking has consequences. These days overweight charges on international flights can be astronomical, which may not bother you but bothers the heck out of me. Even if several hundred dollars in overweight charges doesn't faze you, when you get into African charter flights there may be severe physical limitations on what you can carry. So take what you need, but pack as light as you can. You'll be well taken care of on safari, and you really need a lot less gear than for most hunting trips worldwide.

Now that we've decided what we need to take, it's time to start getting ready for our safari.

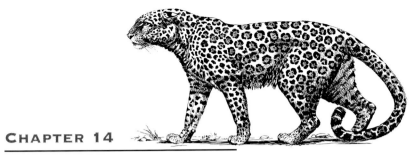

CHAPTER 14

GETTING READY

The dream of Africa lies right around the corner. What can you do to make the most of the experience?

Of the many wonderful things about an African safari, one of the best is the anticipation. Nervousness is natural during the difficult and confusing task of deciding on the right country and choosing your outfitter. A wee touch of buyer's remorse is also natural after you've plunked down a fistful of your hard-earned dollars as a safari deposit. But now that's behind you, and as the months and weeks dwindle only the excitement remains.

Those of us who have been to Africa before may pretend superior knowledge—but we're really jealous of the lucky hunters making their first safari. To the hunter, Africa is not the Dark Continent but the land of enchantment, and the excitement is there, no matter how many times you have visited. But for the first-timer it is a special excitement that will never be equaled—a sense of adventure and the unknown, of long-awaited dreams soon to come true. But in those months, weeks, and days that remain you mustn't spend all of your time daydreaming. There is work to be done . . . and it will only add to the anticipation.

Of course, you will have real work to do as well. I find that I am most productive just before and after a safari—because I have to find some way to pay for it! But you'll have a better experience if you also put some effort into getting ready. There are three areas that can, and should, occupy a fair amount of your time during the months and weeks. These are: studying, getting in shape, and practicing your shooting. Then, in the final days, you must pack carefully and sensibly.

STUDYING

In the business that I'm in, I'm naturally in favor of reading a lot. There is a lot of great African literature, and there are a great many hunting videos. Either medium, or some combination of both, will do two things for you. They will get you ever more excited as your safari draws near; and they will also help prepare you. Hopefully you did some reading and research while making your basic decisions on countries and outfitters; now you can read Africana and watch videos for sheer pleasure and pick up some things along the way.

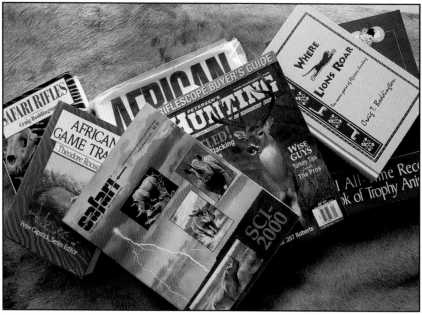

Research is important and a whole lot of fun besides. Good reading, from the old classics to the most current magazines, will help prepare you and will also build anticipation. Just remember that all printed material is dated—and Africa changes.

The basic references remain the same: the *SCI All-time Record Book of Trophy Animals*, James Mellon's *African Hunter*, Robert Ruark, and of course Ernest Hemingway. Keep in mind that Africa is changing fast, and anything written more than a decade ago is out-of-date in terms of specific places and game concentrations. But encounters with African game remain the same, and there is much to be learned from the old masters. There is some very good recent literature as well. I'd like to think that my own stuff has some value, but one of the most useful books ever is *The Perfect Shot* by Kevin (Doctari) Robertson, with anatomical drawings of most African species.

Videos vary tremendously in quality, and many display questionable hunting ethics. There are few that I am truly fond of, but, despite my personal feelings, African hunting videos are invaluable for seeing, as opposed to imagining, what

Elephant hunting also requires a tremendous amount of walking, often dozens of miles a day. Tony Sanchez-Ariño was right when he said, "You hunt elephant with your legs; you execute him with the rifle." In Mozambique the author and his party take a much-needed break before continuing on a track.

227

the country looks like and, of equal importance, what the game really looks like. As you watch the African game, put yourself into the screen and visualize the proper shot placement.

PHYSICAL CONDITION

Don't be afraid of this one. A great deal of African hunting can be enjoyed by the elderly, the very young, people in horrible physical condition, and hunters with severe disabilities. However, I believe you get out of life in full measure what you put into it, and, as is the case with most hunting, you will enjoy Africa more if you are able to fully participate.

Relatively little African hunting is extremely physical. There are exceptions. All mountain hunting is tough. You will have to climb for specialty animals like mountain reedbuck and vaal rhebok, and you will have to climb a great deal for a prize such as mountain nyala. Most hunting in Central Africa is tough. You will walk many miles through the roadless Terminalia forest after Derby eland, and you will walk those miles in incredible heat. You will walk just as many miles through the forest after bongo and the other forest game—and while it won't be as hot in the shade of the forest, you will constantly bend and stoop to get under, over, and through the network of vines that hold you back. For these hunts you really should be in the best physical condition your age and health allow.

Most African hunting requires little more than a bit of walking, usually on good footing but often in fairly warm weather. However, the great and difficult prizes are not the only exceptions. Unless you get lucky, most buffalo hunting takes a good deal of walking, usually several days of following tracks until you come up on the bull you like. Elephant hunting usually requires a great deal more walking than that, though it is really a simple matter of following tracks. You will not catch up every day, and you can't expect that every big set of tracks you follow will have big tusks to match. So you stay at it, day after day, and every day that you see the elephant at the end of the tracks you have won.

Most African hunting takes place during the fall and winter months in the Southern Hemisphere, when the mornings and evenings range from cool to downright cold. The midday temperature swing is considerable, however—and in any tracking hunt you can expect the tracks to take you into the heat of the day, possibly all day. Every hunt is different, and you never know exactly where or how far a track will lead you. Given that you start with fresh spoor, the norm when tracking buffalo is perhaps two to five miles before you can expect to come up on the herd. You will usually have to retrace your steps the same distance in the heat of the day to get back to the track. With elephant, God knows how far you will walk.

The author's vote for the most physical of all African hunting is Lord Derby eland. It's pure tracking in country with very few roads, and even in winter the equatorial region gets extremely hot.

But I know this: If you're in shape to walk twenty miles a day, day after day, you are far more likely to find a big tusker!

If you can't do that, there are other options. You can wait at water holes, or you can take only smoking-fresh tracks and then break off when you approach your limit. This is not a problem; hunting is supposed to be fun, and it's no fun to push yourself beyond your personal limits. It's also unhealthy and unsafe. But the more ground you can cover without hurting yourself, the better your chances for big trophies.

Tracking is a traditional African hunting technique that goes beyond the big stuff. Depending on the area, the game, and the professional hunter, you can get into some surprisingly long tracking jobs with zebra and any of the larger antelope, including roan, sable, kudu, and especially eland. But, except for eland, lengthy tracking is relatively unusual with most plains game. More often, you will hunt plains game by spotting and stalking, or perhaps by making a relatively short still-hunt through likely cover, such as walking a riverbank for bushbuck in the late afternoon. Rarely will such walking require more than a mile or two. However, if you mess things up and have to follow a wounded animal, there is no telling how far even an impala might take you!

Most African hunting, at its best, purest, and most enjoyable, requires walking. These days, regrettably, there are quite a few "truck hunters" around, and there are even some well-known professional hunters who boast that their clients rarely have to walk. If you can't walk, that's one thing. If you can, then I think you're robbing yourself of the best part of the African experience by using the vehicle more than is necessary. Stalking your game on foot, getting close, and setting up a good shot is part of the adventure and makes some of the best memories.

The good news is that the only way to get into shape for walking is to walk, which isn't all that tough a thing to do. There is no African hunting that requires anyone to be in pentathlon condition. Only under very rare conditions does the client have to pack meat or anything else. These days it is more normal for you to carry your own rifle than to have someone else carry it, but if you get tired, one of the trackers will gladly carry it. All the trackers ask is that you be with them at the end of the track, which means you should be in shape to walk for several hours at a relatively slow pace. This may be asking a lot in extreme heat, but if you build up until you can walk three or four miles without being a basket case, you can handle most African hunting.

Again, walking is the best preparation. I'm not a talented runner, but I'm a fairly consistent runner. Running and walking don't use the same muscles in the same way, and if I forget to take some conditioning hikes before a hunt, I wind

The standing or offhand position is the most difficult and should be a last resort in the field; but sometimes, especially in thick cover, you must stand up and shoot. The only answer is lots and lots of practice.

up with sore muscles—even if I've maintained my running regimen! So do some walking, and do it in the shoes or boots you plan on taking on safari.

You will make a lot of brownie points with your crew if you help load the game and help push if the vehicle gets stuck, but very little heavy work is expected of the safari client. Of course, hunting is hunting. There are many situations where you must make a mad dash to get a shot, so being in good shape is definitely an advantage. If you can run fifty or a hundred yards and then shoot without your heart pounding out of your chest, you will get more shots than the person who can't. Most African hunting, even when done right, is not nearly as physical as much North American hunting, but you will enjoy it much more if you take a few hours a week to get in the best condition you can.

SHOOTING PRACTICE

To my mind, shooting practice is the most important preparation of all. African game has a somewhat undeserved reputation for being tougher than game elsewhere. And Africa has dangerous game that doesn't exist elsewhere. Because of these two factors, all too many clients show up with unfamiliar rifles and don't shoot particularly well. It's OK to take "new" rifles on safari, but it's not OK to be unfamiliar with them. Familiarity means much more than just sighting-in and packing the gun case.

Worldwide, every professional hunter I know complains bitterly about the shooting competence of the average client. Although the problems are many, three complaints come to the fore. First, especially in Africa, too many hunters bring powerful rifles that they are afraid of. Second, relatively few hunters can shoot well from improvised rests or unsteady field positions. Third, while the skill to shoot may well be present, many hunters have trouble getting their shots off quickly enough.

The author gets one of Remington's new Ultra Mags ready for a trip to Tanzania. The bench is the best place to make sure your rifle is zeroed and to find out how well it shoots and what ammo it likes—but the bench is poor practice for real field shooting.

Recoil is always a factor, and shooting on the range "in cold blood" accentuates it. A standing rest like this, used to regulate double rifles, minimizes felt recoil and also offers a good starting point for field-shooting positions.

There is no question that recoil is a serious problem. You need powerful rifles for Africa's largest game, but you aren't doing anybody any good by taking a rifle on safari that you are afraid to shoot. With enough recoil-dampening gun weight and proper stock fit, most people can learn to shoot fairly powerful rifles, but everyone has a different recoil threshold. The only answer is to be honest with yourself. If you simply can't handle a hard-kicking big-bore or a fast-kicking medium, then you probably need a .270 or a .30-06 for the plains game and a ten-pound .375 for the big stuff. In the previous chapter we talked a lot about appropriate guns and loads, and every statement was valid. But this is also valid: There is no safari in Africa that can't be handled with a .30-06 and a .375, and everyone can learn to shoot these cartridges.

Get as much shooting practice as you possibly can. The problem, I think, is that too many of us do the wrong kind of practice. The benchrest is a wonderful tool for sighting-in your rifle, and it is equally useful for learning what loads your rifle likes and how accurate it really is. However, the benchrest is absolutely useless in improving your field shooting skills. There will be no benchrest in Africa.

You need to get away from the bench and practice from the kinds of positions you might actually use in the field. In my experience, this means positions that are a bit different from those common in North America. I personally like the sitting position, but in Africa brush and grass are often too tall, so you need to get higher. It is extremely common for one of the trackers to carry a bamboo tripod, which makes a wonderful rest. But no rest is easy to use if you haven't practiced with it. So make yourself a tripod and learn how to use it. I have also done a great deal of African hunting leaning against a tree or over a tree limb. And, when stalking, I've done a lot more shooting just plain offhand— standing up—than I have anywhere else in the world. Offhand is the most difficult of all shooting positions, and few of us practice it. This is a big mistake. Offhand, as the most difficult, should be practiced the most—even though you should avoid it in the field if you have a choice.

I can't tell you how much you should shoot before going on safari. This depends on how much shooting experience you have in the first place. I can tell you that you can't acquire a lifetime of experience in two or three sessions at the range. And if you try to "cram," you'll probably overdo it, and recoil, even if moderate, will start to get to you. A really good session at the range is probably not more than twenty centerfire cartridges fired downrange from a variety of positions. With cartridges of .375 H&H power and greater, cut that in half. A session like this, every week for three or four months, will yield far greater benefit than trying to pump a hundred rounds downrange in one day.

It is important to do a lot of shooting with the rifle or rifles you're actually taking to Africa, but don't limit yourself to them. The best teaching tool, and the best way to become a good rifle shot, is a good old .22 rimfire. Ammo cost is low, noise is minimal,

The author's buddy, Chub Eastman of Nosler Bullets, has done a lot of African hunting, but he's also an extremely avid varmint hunter. Maybe that's why he's one of the best field marksmen.

Radical temperature changes are common in much of Africa, so don't forget to pack some warm clothes. The author wears heavy wool sweaters a lot in the mornings and evenings. Sometimes that isn't enough, so throw in a wind-breaking jacket and some gloves.

and recoil is nil. You can shoot a .22 to your heart's content, and you can shoot it from all manner of field positions. It remains the best training tool there is, and time spent with a .22 is never wasted.

In Africa, speed is important. You are often dealing with herd animals, in contrast to most North American situations. When the chosen animal steps clear, you must shoot. The same is true for shooting in thornbush or woodland, which is no different from shooting at whitetails in thick cover. You must find a window through the vegetation, and when the animal is there you must get your shot off. Good whitetail hunters do pretty well in Africa's thornbush and woodlands, but many Americans are too deliberate and too slow to take the shot that is offered.

This is a very hard skill to learn, and it is even harder in the typical rifle range situation where you have all the time in the world. Forget about the time, and practice getting into a shooting position and firing quickly. Again, a lot of time with a .22 is very valuable. Watching hunting videos or wildlife shows on TV is also valuable. Watch the animals move in and out of

At the airport, en route to a three-week safari in C.A.R. On most African hunts you can get by with a mid-sized duffel bag, a carry-on bag, and your gun case. Pay special attention to the carry-on, packing it as if it is the only bag you will receive.

the shadows. Concentrate on finding the shoulder quickly, judging the angle of presentation, and visualize yourself getting the shot off. This kind of mental exercise is not as good as actual field experience, but it might well be the next-best thing.

PACKING TIPS

Part of the fun in preparing for any safari is laying out all the gear (over and over again) and making sure you have everything you need, then seeing if it will fit and how it fits best. This is a healthy exercise, but it's best to go as light as you can. This is not only because the airlines have gone nuts on overweight baggage charges; most tents, rondavels, or whatever the accommodations are, have very limited room for storage of gear. Your sleeping quarters will be far more orderly and it will be easier to find things if you don't bring more than you need.

I prefer a duffel bag for my gear, and of course a good, sturdy, hard gun case for the firearms. Check with your airline regarding any specific requirements for packing ammunition, because this is subject to change. In most cases the ammo must be separate from the firearms, and some airlines are firm about requiring a locked wood or metal container. The "five-kilogram limit" is fairly standard. Usually I put my ammunition in a padlocked military surplus ammo can, then put the ammo can in the center of my duffel bag.

The single most important packing tip is this: Take a generous carry-on bag. I always pack a day pack, and it stays with me throughout the safari. Whatever bag you choose, pack your carry-on luggage as if your checked baggage will not arrive! This has only happened to me once, but it does happen. You can buy underwear, clothes, and sundries in virtually any African city. You can borrow a rifle in any hunting camp. What you cannot readily replace are: medications, binoculars, camera, extra eyeglasses or contact lenses, comfortable shoes you can hunt in, and a jacket to keep you from freezing your tail in the morning cold. If you arrive with these things in your carry-on bag, your safari can proceed, whether your checked baggage arrives or not. It probably will, but don't check anything that you absolutely cannot do without!

PART IV

GETTING THE MOST
OUT OF YOUR SAFARI

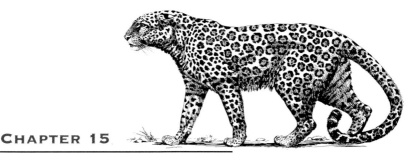

CHAPTER 15

SHOOTING AND SHOT PLACEMENT

None of us is perfect, but you'll shoot better if you know what to expect.

Robert Ruark's *Horn of the Hunter* is one of the very best African books—in my mind the best "first safari" book, even more enjoyable than Hemingway's *Green Hills of Africa*. Ruark, unlike all too many of us, doesn't mind poking fun at himself, and in the early stages of that long-ago safari he had an incredible case of "missitis." The professional hunter Harry Selby consoled him by telling him that everybody missed at first. "Something different about the light." Yeah, sure it was the light.

Ruark actually had a pretty good excuse. Although he'd wanted to go to Africa since boyhood, until the first day of his very first safari he was primarily a shotgunner. He had an impressive battery of fine rifles with him, and I assume he had done some shooting on the range. But I seriously doubt he had done much of the kind of practice I talked about in the last chapter—off the bench and from genuine field positions. Rifle shooting is different from shotgunning, but once they get the hang of it shotgunners tend to make good field riflemen. So it's no more surprising that Ruark eventually did very well than it is that he missed a lot at first. At least he had a good excuse . . . and it wasn't because Africa's light is different!

Regardless what excuse you manage to come up with, it isn't uncommon for first-time African hunters to start out

The author had another serious case of "missitis" on this hunt in Tanzania in 1988. He couldn't remember how many times he shot at this tommy before he finally connected! These things happen, and you simply have to work your way through it.

shooting badly. I did it on my first safari, and, if I must admit it, I've had bouts of missitis much more recently. Which suggests that, sooner or later, I'll probably have this dread malady again. Provided you practice sensibly and not so much that you make yourself flinchy, there's no such thing as too much shooting practice—especially if you're starting with unfamiliar rifles, or if you don't have a great deal of field experience to begin with. Only through practice can you gain confidence, and only with confidence can you shoot well when you're excited, nervous, or just plain scared. However, it is important to understand that even with all the practice in the world, all the confidence in the world, and all the shooting skill in the world, you are going to miss sooner or later.

Can't happen to you? Sure it can. Nobody's perfect. Hunters who say they have never missed have limited field

Most professional hunters will insist on checking the rifles before starting to hunt, not only to ensure zero but also to evaluate how well they shoot. Travel is hard on rifles, so if a PH doesn't insist, you should!

experience or very selective memories. And never forget that wonderful line about "pride goeth before a fall." Every professional hunter in Africa has stories about clients who came in boasting about their shooting or saying things like, "Just show 'em to me and I can hit 'em." Lady Luck does have a sense of humor, and she is almost sure to strike out if you give her this kind of an opening. Practice as much as you can, and become as familiar and proficient with your rifles as you can. Then be honest with your professional hunter, because he will ask what kind of shots you are comfortable taking. If you think you're really good, tell him you'll probably be OK on reasonable shots. If you don't know, tell him that. But don't boast and don't lie. He'll probably have you check your rifles on the first day, and he'll form his own opinion no matter what you tell him!

And be prepared to miss. The light isn't necessarily different, but Africa is different—and you are different while you're there. If it's your first safari, you have dreamed of this moment and saved for it for a very long time. Of course you're nervous, because all those dreams and all that work ride on that very first shot. Except they don't. Do the best you can, accept that you won't shoot perfectly every time, and remember that you're not whitetail hunting in the eastern United States. If you miss, there will be another chance tomorrow. This is important to remember because, at least in my experience, one miss breeds another. You know you can make a shot, but you blow it. You brood on it, and your concentration is shattered. So one miss becomes two or three or more! It's difficult to do, but if you miss a shot you simply must put it out of your mind and go on to the next opportunity, whether the same day or a couple of days later. On the common game there will be another opportunity. On the tough stuff, well, sometimes that's the way it goes. Just forget about it and keep hunting.

Do not make a mental decision to try harder. Chances are you were trying as hard as you could, but you were too nervous or too slow or you misread the body position, or whatever. If you try harder you'll probably be trying too hard, and you'll be all clenched up, which leads to missitis. Just forget about it and keep hunting. You'll get over it, and so will your professional hunter. Except for this: If you really and truly have no clue as to why you missed, or how you could have missed, stop hunting immediately and go check your rifle. If your scope was off, you'll feel better immediately knowing the miss wasn't your fault. Chances are the scope wasn't off and it was your fault. That's OK; you need to know that, too, and it's easier to forget about it if you aren't left to wonder.

Misses are part of safari life, and you must learn to deal with them. Most of the time they really will be your fault, but you must start every safari with a clean slate by ensuring that your

The legend is that African game is extra tough, but this is relative. Many antelope, like this impala, are much smaller than American deer. As long as you're using a rifle that would be adequate for whitetail, "toughness" is really a moot point.

Some African antelope, like the wildebeest, deserve their reputation for extreme toughness. This is where there is no substitute for shot placement. The author's wife Bernadette, not an experienced hunter, dropped this bull cleanly with one well-placed shot from her little .260 Remington.

rifles haven't shifted to zero during the long journey. Most experienced professional hunters will absolutely insist on this, but some PHs just aren't gun guys, so if they don't insist, you must. Airplane trips really aren't that hard on rifles, and I haven't had to adjust my sights that often, but there have been a few occasions when the sights were way, way out. You simply must check.

And, again, if you miss a shot that you honestly feel you should have made, better check again. Clear back in 1979 Barrie Duckworth and I were having really bad luck with sable. Most of it was my fault. I'm a western hunter, not an eastern whitetail hunter, and I was having a tough time in Rhodesia's mopane woodlands. Barrie finally got me in on the biggest sable I have ever seen before or since. We got a very clean shot in open mopanes, and I missed him clean. More than once. To tell you the truth, I didn't shoot very well that whole safari, and I don't know why. But that time I knew it wasn't my fault. So we backed off and checked the rifle. It was 18 inches high at less than one hundred yards. There was a ding on the front bell of the scope that I hadn't noticed, perhaps from riding in the truck.

We readjusted the scope, retraced our steps, and later that day got back into the same herd. This time I made a perfect shot . . . except that I shot the wrong sable. We'll talk about that later. The main thing is that you should always check your rifle if you can't explain a miss. Come to think of it, you should check it more often than that. On most safaris, certainly most "first safaris," you will be shooting the rifle at least every day or two. But on the tough hunts, such as bongo and Derby eland, you may hunt hard for several days without firing a shot. If you've been walking a lot in tough country, if the rifle has gotten wet, or especially if one of the trackers has been carrying it, it's a good idea to take a test shot every few days. You may not get more than one shot at the great prizes, and you need to know that your rifle is on.

When you check your rifles on the first day of your safari, you can be sure that your professional hunter is evaluating your abilities. He's looking at not only how well you shoot but how safe you are. I don't know about you, but I'm real nervous around strangers with guns. So don't be offended if your PH asks you to check your chamber now and then, or tells you to watch where your muzzle is pointed. You should be watching these things even if he isn't. It's perfectly OK to watch his gun muzzle as well. Gun safety applies in Africa just like everywhere else, and all too many PHs have lost their lives to unsafe gun handling.

Let's get to the actual shooting business. Your PH will probably ask you what distance you are comfortable shooting and how you like to shoot. You may or may not know, but tell him what you know, or tell him that you don't know. If you've practiced offhand a great deal and are comfortable with

This is the position the author was in when he shot his western greater kudu in Chad, about two hundred yards from an unsupported sitting position. The more shooting positions you have practiced from and are comfortable with, the greater the diversity of shots you can handle.

The brush often makes it impossible to use anything except a standing, unsupported shooting position. No one can do this from long range, but you should be able to stand up and shoot accurately out to at least seventy-five yards or so.

that, tell him. If you are uncomfortable shooting without a rest, tell him that as well. As I mentioned in the previous chapter, the normal African expedient is to make a tripod of three fairly straight poles about six feet long. Typically, the lead tracker carries the tripod, and if a shot seems imminent he will spread the legs, set it down, and move out of your way. Your action is to step forward, lay the fore-end over the top, and shoot when the proper animal is identified. This is actually very fast and effective, and I highly recommend it, especially in open country where tree limbs and other natural rests are scarce.

However, like all shooting positions and shooting rests, the tripod takes some getting used to. The height needs to be right, and you have to figure out how to rest the rifle and settle your body in behind it. If you're going to use a tripod, practice with it a bit around camp, not necessarily shooting but just getting into position and steadying the rifle.

Tripods, or shooting sticks, are often used in Africa. They're wonderful, but they take some getting used to. You can practice at home by simply tying three poles together.

If some positions or shots are problematic for you, tell your PH. If you don't know your strong and weak points, don't worry about it. This will become apparent as your safari progresses. For instance, I have a terrible time shooting from a vehicle. I know it's legal in a lot of areas, but it's so ingrained in me that this is wrong that I have a mental block about it. I used to fight it, but now I simply tell my PHs that I can't shoot from the vehicle. If they don't believe me, I usually don't have any trouble proving it!

When actually shooting at game, the first and most important rule is never, ever to shoot unless the PH tells you to. Whenever possible, an experienced professional hunter will get you into a good shooting position, and then he will evaluate the game and make a "shoot/don't shoot" decision. It is always possible that you see something that he does not, but only remotely possible. The best rule of thumb, again, is never shoot unless the PH tells you to. It's not only a matter of allowing the PH time to judge trophy quality. African hunting is different from many situations in that you are often faced with herds. In poor light—such as midday shadows in the woodlands—it can be very difficult to sort out the buffalo bulls from the cows, the eland bulls from the cows, the sable and roan bulls from the cows. They all have horns. Even in the best light it takes a lot of experience to sort oryx bulls from cows, zebra stallions from mares, and so forth. Not to mention the nightmare of picking the best bull from a herd of several hundred lechwe bulls! You not only have to sort out the correct animal but you also have to make sure that animal presents a clear target, without another animal directly behind.

Never shoot without your PH's approval, but make absolutely certain that you understand what he is telling you. Some circumstances make this very difficult, such as in a big herd of lechwe or oryx. Come to think of it, excitement and pressure make it difficult even when it should not be. Back to that sable. I was not yet twenty-seven on that safari, and I didn't know nearly as much as I thought I did. Barrie Duckworth, one of Zimbabwe's truly great modern-day professional hunters, was guiding his very first client after leaving the Rhodesian game department. We were both pretty green. We were on a little ridge, looking down into a leafy *korango* where the herd of sable was milling about. We found the bull, I guess. I saw a sable move behind a tree, and Barrie said, "The big bull is behind that tree." A sable came out, and I shot, hammering it in its tracks. Then Barrie pointed out the big bull running up out of the draw. Oooops!

At the time I was unable to accept that it was my fault. Actually, it was. Barrie had only told me the bull was behind that tree; I was tremendously excited, and I misinterpreted the message. He never told me to shoot. I doubt he will ever forget that day, any more than I will, so today he might say things like, "Don't shoot until I tell you!" After that experience (and others), that is what I tell hunters when I'm doing the guiding! So there are really two principles: The first is never to shoot until the PH gives his approval, and the second is to make sure you understand what he is telling you. That sable was a straightforward mistake. It gets more complex when you're dealing with a big herd, but you and your PH simply must sort it out before you fire.

If you're counting from left to right or right to left, make sure you have the same starting point. Take the time and talk it over if you must, but get it right. It is far, far better to pass a shot than to make a mistake. Having said that, let's talk about the third related principle. I've already said that we're all going to miss. That is true, and since there are various degrees of missing, it is also true that we're all going to wound game sooner or later. Unpleasant as it is, this is part of hunting and it will happen; but you don't need to help the law of averages along the way. Do not take any shot unless you are reasonably certain you can make a solid, mortal hit. It is far better to let it go. There may be another opportunity at that animal, and even if there isn't, there will be another day.

From the standpoint of proper sportsmanship and hunting ethics, you don't want to make a mistake. Altruism aside, you still don't want to make a mistake. Under some circumstances a mistake will merely be costly, because you will have to pay a second trophy fee (or, in some cases, a double trophy fee for a female). In other cases the cost is the entire safari. A good example is Ethiopia. Just as in the United States, you must purchase a license up front, one specimen of a given species per customer; and, just as in the rest of Africa, a drop of blood is a filled tag. I know three or four good hunters who have wounded and lost mountain nyala in the high heather of Ethiopia, which is unusual because I know very few people who have hunted mountain nyala! Knowing this, and aware that a twenty-one-day safari (with almost no other game) rested on the shot, I was extremely nervous when I made a

Much is made over exactly where to shoot the various unfamiliar game animals. Studying pictures and diagrams helps, but game animals are much the same the world over. If you shoot this buffalo squarely on the center of the shoulder with a good bullet from an adequate rifle, it will be just as dead as any smaller animal would be.

decision to shoot my big bull in March 2000. I was over a tripod and I had confidence in the rifle, and the mountain nyala dropped in its tracks. But it was a shot worth thinking about before leaping into it—and so is almost any shot in Africa (or anywhere else).

Some time back we talked about African game country. It varies, encompassing plains, deserts, mountains, woodlands, forests, and swamps, so it is altogether impossible to characterize the kind of shooting you might expect on the "typical" safari. Also, it depends on what you're used to. I'm comfortable with fairly long shooting in open country, because that's where I grew up. I had trouble just plain seeing game, let alone shooting, in heavy thornbush and woodland. The shadows confounded me, and I had a terrible time locating a "window" to shoot through, even when the game was quite visible. An eastern whitetail hunter would probably thrive under such conditions, where shooting is rarely more than a hundred yards but the shot must be timed as the animal moves through the undergrowth. I got used to it, but it took several safaris. I am still trying to get used to the true forest, where distances shrink from yards to feet. A hunter from the rainforests of the Pacific Northwest would probably feel right at home.

On the other hand, I feel comfortable and confident in the open savannas, deserts, and mountains, where close shots are two hundred yards. An experienced eastern whitetail hunter will feel just as uncomfortable there as I feel when shots come at bayonet range.

I am not recommending choosing the African country most similar to the hunting you're used to. Not at all. Your choice depends entirely on where the game you want to hunt is located. The point is that African hunting may present situations that are reasonably familiar or altogether unfamiliar. Keep an open mind, and prepare yourself for the most varied situations possible. And no matter how you practice, and wherever you plan to hunt, keep in mind that one of the most important things in field shooting is speed. This doesn't mean shooting before you (and your PH) are certain of the target. It does mean that African game is under constant pressure from predators great and small. Most species are considerably more nervous than our domestic game, and opportunities for the ideal shot are fleeting. You must learn how to get positioned quickly—and you must do that long before you arrive in Africa. Then you must find a way to get in sync with your PH, so that you understand his directions and know exactly where he's looking and pointing. And then you must be able to take advantage of the best shot when it presents itself.

None of this is easy, and none of us will get it right all the time. But the more preparation you have, the better off you will be. My old friend Matt Daniel, a western hunter who had used telescopic sights for years, was headed to Africa and planned to use his open-sighted .460 Weatherby for elephant and buffalo. There's a little valley behind the house on his ranch, filled with California live oaks. Matt festooned the branches with empty pill bottles, then practiced offhand with the big .460 until he could hit a pill bottle at thirty or forty yards every time he mounted the rifle. Extreme? Maybe. Except that he took a lion charge head-on, and brained the lion with the big .460. His widow, Rachelann, who was with him at the time, has the lion skull with a .460-size hole between the eyes.

More recently, I've been watching my friend Marshal Kaplan prepare for his first safari. Marshal knows a great deal about rifles but has little field experience. I was there a couple of years ago when he shot his first game animal, a California wild hog. He shot perfectly, partly because he had practiced a great deal and partly because he listened. Lately he's spent several sessions at the range practicing with his .375 H&H and .470 Rigby from all manner of field positions. He still doesn't have a great deal of field experience, but he knows how to shoot those big rifles, and I'm pretty sure he still knows how to listen. I'll be surprised if he doesn't do extremely well.

Now, in terms of actual shot placement, I don't think there's a great deal of mystery. African game is not bulletproof, and, despite the legend, I don't think African game is necessarily tougher than our domestic game. It depends on the animal and what you're comparing it to. American elk are extremely tough, but our deer are not. Greater kudu, although large, are not particularly tough. Wildebeest are extremely tough, as are sable and roan. As I've written before, I think it's a moot point whether impala-sized game are tough or not; if you choose sensibly, your light rifle will be quite adequate for overcoming innate toughness. As is the case everywhere in the world and on all varieties of game, the secret is to get the bullet into the right place. If your cartridge is reasonably adequate, your bullet is tough enough to reach the vitals, and if you direct that bullet properly so that it reaches the vitals, the question of toughness should not arise.

Ah, but where should you place the shot to accomplish all of this? It is a good exercise to study mounted specimens, animals in zoos, and anatomical drawings. As mentioned previously, Kevin Robertson's *The Perfect Shot* is a wonderful reference for anatomically correct drawings. However, it is unreasonable to expect yourself to memorize the anatomy of the twenty-odd animals you might encounter, most of which you have never before seen in the flesh. It is even more unreasonable to expect your game to stand around while you pull out drawings and do some crash studying before shooting. There are some simple rules you can follow.

Most Americans prefer the lung shot, right behind the shoulder, because it offers the largest target, is definitely fatal, and damages little meat. The correct placement of the perfect

Gun safety is just as important in Africa as it is everywhere else. Train yourself to watch where the muzzle is pointed, and if you hand your rifle off to someone else to carry, make absolutely certain the chamber is empty.

lung shot varies a bit with the different African species, and a shot that is a wee bit high or a wee bit back in the lungs can yield a long tracking job. Most professional hunters prefer the shoulder shot, and I agree with them. Take a broadside animal and divide it horizontally into thirds. Now take the central line of the foreleg and follow it up into the body. Place your shot along this line in the upper portion of the bottom horizontal third. This is the central shoulder shot. The exact location of the heart also varies from species to species, but, provided the bullet is tough enough to penetrate the shoulder, there is no animal in the world, from elephant on down, that can survive this shot or that will go far from such a shot.

Sure, there are pitfalls. The primary one is that game animals have the option to stand facing any one of the 360 degrees of the compass, so genuine broadside shots are relatively rare. You have to read the angle and adjust your hold accordingly. Always visualize that the heart lies fairly low in the chest cavity between the shoulders. Regardless of the angle, that's the spot you're trying to reach. If that spot is obscured, the lung shot is also good. On a broadside animal, just follow the rear line of the foreleg up into the bottom half of the central horizontal third.

Again, studying pictures and drawings is good; studying three-dimensional animals—mounted or live specimens in zoos—is better. But don't get fancy. It took Karamojo Bell a long time to master the brain shot on elephant! If you don't have a clear shot at the heart or lung area—in that order—or you aren't certain exactly how to get your bullet there, it's far better to pass the shot.

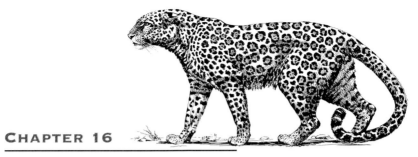

CHAPTER 16

DO ALL YOU CAN—BUT NOT TOO MUCH

It's easy to get sidetracked in Africa. For best results, set your goals and stick to them!

No other continent can match the diversity of Africa's wildlife. Think of it. More than one hundred varieties of antelope, plus the cats, buffalo, zebra, pig, elephant, and more. In perspective, however, Africa's landmass is huge, second only to Asia. As we have seen, many of Africa's species are quite localized, while others are widespread—but you won't hunt them all on one safari, or on ten safaris.

Most hunting areas offer variety that will be unprecedented in your hunting experience. A very specialized area may offer potential for only a half-dozen different trophies, but there are a few parts of Africa where you might find twenty huntable species in the same general vicinity. In your search for the right outfitter and area, you probably studied a whole bunch of seductive brochures. Each one had a game list, some very long and some fairly short. It is even possible that you based your selection, at least in part, on the list of available game. There's nothing wrong with this, but it must be understood in context.

Since outfitters' game lists are sales tools, most are quite complete. They tend to contain not only the common animals that most hunters encounter but the locally rare animals that will be seen only occasionally. Either way, accept at the outset that on one safari you will not ship home representatives of every species included on the outfitter's game list. Some species you probably will not even see, and others you will

Some animals, like the warthog, are often extremely common, but you won't see many good trophies. If you want a big warthog, you take one when you see him.

see but not take, perhaps for lack of shooting opportunity and perhaps for lack of trophy quality. That doesn't mean that game lists are false advertising. Game lists tell the prospective hunter what game is present and what might be encountered, and it lists the trophy and/or license fees. This is invaluable information, because you need to know what you're in for when you squeeze the trigger, and there isn't always time to talk about it and count pennies when an opportunity arises. But don't expect that you will take all the animals you have contracted to hunt and have put on your wish list. It can happen, but it won't happen all the time. By the way, modern game quotas are small and carefully allocated, and at the time you book the safari you should put on your list any animal you wish to hunt. Other animals might be available, but if you didn't put it down in writing at time of booking, don't count on it!

The sitatunga is another very specialized hunt. This animal may be the primary objective of a shorter safari, or you may devote several days of a longer hunt to it. Either way, there is little other game in the swamps.

There are too many variables to predict exactly how much game anyone might take on a given safari. The competence of both professional hunter and client enter the picture, as does the degree of selectivity. Most first-time hunters are quite happy with representative trophies. Their bags will be larger than those of veteran hunters who are trying to improve on trophies already taken, or who settle for nothing less than exceptional trophies. Rain or lack thereof is often a factor, and it also depends on how difficult the primary species turn out to be, and how much time you spend hunting them.

As a rule of thumb, it wouldn't be unusual for a hunter in a good area holding a diversity of game to average about one trophy for every day and a half of hunting. So a good bag would be about seven trophies for a ten-day safari, about ten trophies for a two-week safari, and perhaps fourteen for a three-week safari. Two hunters sharing a guide on a two-to-one basis won't do quite as well, but, provided both hunters are fairly competent and everyone works together, each hunter will have similar results. That's what you wanted to hear, right? Just how much game can you really expect to take on your first safari? I first read almost exactly the same formula in an agent's brochure some twenty-five years ago, when I was planning my first safari. It was fairly accurate back then, and it remains fairly accurate today.

There is a big, important "except": This formula works pretty well, but it doesn't speak to the more difficult prizes that most hunters consider important, nor does it speak to priorities. There is a tremendous variety of game in most African hunting areas. Most hunters, especially on their first several safaris, do indeed take quite a few trophies—almost certainly more than they have ever taken on any single hunting

In southern Africa you will usually see impala several times a day, so you can take your time and be selective. Sooner or later you'll see the one you want. (Photo: Safari Press library)

trip in their lives. But it's almost unheard of to take all of the animals on a given outfitter's game list—and, whether you do or not, it's far more important to take the animals that are most important to you. Because of Africa's great variety, it's easy to get sidetracked, and if you do that you run the risk of finishing the safari with a large and varied bag of wonderful trophies but without the trophies most important to you.

It's no different anywhere else in the world. There are lots of "combination hunts" in the American West that include both elk and mule deer. Most sportsmen on such hunts concentrate on elk, and, whether they're successful or not, relatively few fill their deer tags. This is because there may be good deer country nearby, but ideal elk country is not ideal deer country. Time is limited, and most of it is devoted to the target with a high payoff. Last year two buddies and I went on a two-week combination in the Yukon. All seasons were open—sheep, moose, caribou, grizzly, black bear, wolf, wolverine. By North American standards this is an incredible variety of game. We all had tags for everything, and we all harbored secret dreams of a "full bag." Dall sheep was the primary quarry for all of us, and we all took very good rams. After that we moved into lower country and looked for other game. But it was still early in a warm fall, that period purposefully selected to give us the best chance for sheep. We hunted our tails off. I took a good caribou, one partner took a nice grizzly, and we all passed up reasonable moose—but no other tags were filled. So if we judged the trip by how many tags were filled in relation to how many tags we had in our pockets, the trip was a failure. None of us judged it that way. Sheep was most important, and we all got very fine rams. We judged it one of the best hunts any of us had been on.

In Africa there is such great variety that most likely you will take some variety of game along the way, but priorities are just as important, maybe more so. On a first African hunt you

In greater kudu country a big bull may pop up anywhere. You can hunt for them specifically, and you probably will if you want a kudu; but many big bulls are taken through chance encounter. Gary Williams took this monster in Zambia.

may not have strong preferences and priorities. If you don't, that's wonderful. You can go and have a great time and take each day as it comes. At the end of the safari the skinning shed will probably be full, and you will have had a wonderful time. But most of us do have priorities. Maybe it's a big kudu or a buffalo, or maybe it's one of the cats. If there are certain trophies you really want, you should hunt hard for them and not worry too much about how quickly the trophy shed is filling up.

As I've said before, I don't personally recommend hunting either lion or leopard on a first safari. This is because cat hunting is a single-minded and time-consuming pursuit. In most circumstances the first thing that needs to happen is to get baits hung. In today's Africa, quotas and bag limits are restrictive enough that there are few "extra" bait animals; both bait animals and camp meat count against your license, and two of a given species on license is increasingly rare. So you'll spend the first few days of your hunt looking for fresh cat tracks, taking some common species for bait along the way. This means that looking for bait animals and serious trophy hunting aren't a good mix, especially if you find smoking-fresh pug marks and need a bait quickly.

Once the baits are hung they must be checked daily. They will probably be a long distance apart, so most of the morning hunt will be spent dashing from one end of the area to the other to see if the baits have been hit. Sure, you can do some hunting along the way, but if you spend several hours tracking buffalo or following a kudu you've seen, you may not get to the one bait that you must get to.

Once you get a hit you will build a blind and perhaps freshen the bait, and then your schedule is set. If you are hunting leopard you may sit in the blind only in the evening, but in some areas that means most of the night. If you are hunting lion, you may sit in the blind both morning and evening. With lion the morning is the most likely, but you never know. If you get the cat, then you can go on to hunt other things. The reality, however, is that you may sit in one blind or another throughout the safari . . . and success is not assured. You should understand this going in, so if you really concentrate on the cat and fail there will be no hard feelings. Neither lion nor leopard is ever a sure thing.

However, if you have done your research well and have found a good hunter and a good area, you probably will be successful in getting your cat, if you put in the time. This is very hard to do on a first safari. Sure, you booked the hunt with a big cat in mind, but Africa is all new, and most first-timers want to experience as much of it as possible. So you get carried away, hunting kudu, spooring buffalo, even hunting the common game. This is all great stuff, and you should do as much as you can on a first safari—but if you do, you are seriously hurting your chances of getting the cat.

Based on hard and expensive experience, I think it's much better to leave the cats out of a first safari, unless you can afford to book a lengthy safari of no less than three weeks into one of the really great general-bag areas—Zambia, Tanzania, or Botswana. If you can do that, then you will probably have time to hunt the cats properly along with everything else. Still, you won't fill the entire game list, and the cats are not a sure thing.

My first safari was a three-week hunt in Kenya, with lion as the primary goal. I took a wonderful selection of game, but I never got a lion. In this particular circumstance I don't think it was because I got sidetracked; we turned down two nearly maneless males late in the hunt, and I don't believe the kind of lion I was looking for existed in the blocks I was hunting at that time. I was terribly disappointed, primarily because I had set myself up for failure. I'd have been far better off saving the lion for a later trip.

There were later trips for lion that also failed. Partly it was because I wasn't in the best lion country, and partly it was because I was hunting new country with lots of unfamiliar species, and I let myself get sidetracked time and again. My luck didn't turn until I hunted good country in Zambia in 1983. I have actually had worse luck with leopard. Over the years I have hung many baits and built and sat in many blinds, but most of this effort was haphazard, while I was hunting other things. I shot a leopard almost by accident in Botswana in 1985, but the only leopard I ever saw properly come to a bait was in Zimbabwe in 1992, on the fourteenth day of the only safari that I have truly devoted to leopard hunting.

Lion and leopard are not the only examples of game that require concentrated effort. On a typical ten-day buffalo hunt, your time is limited. Most professional hunters will start such a hunt by seriously pursuing buffalo. Sure, you may take an impala or a warthog along the way,

This is a Nigerian bohor reedbuck, but most of the several races are found in microhabitats of heavy grass. Some grassy swales hold reedbuck, but most do not. Most reedbuck are taken incidentally when you happen to be in the right place at the right time.

Almost all areas have indigenous species not found elsewhere. They may be easy to hunt, like these black lechwe in Bangweulu, or very difficult. You may never return to that area, so pay attention to the local rarities wherever you are hunting.

and you will take a really good kudu whenever you see it—but you won't consciously look for other game until your buffalo trophy is in the skinning shed. If everything goes well, this should be a matter of three to five days, depending on how picky you are. But it might take a week or more, and there wouldn't be much time to take other game. If a buffalo is what you want, stick with it. If you give up, you can probably take a half-dozen other trophies—but you wanted a buffalo, and you'll be much more satisfied with the safari if you see it through.

Virtually all of the high-profile antelope—kudu, sable, roan, eland, nyala, waterbuck—can be time-consuming to

Tracking hunts are almost always time-consuming. This is a bongo track, and few hunts are more intensive or specialized. Because you will hunt mostly on foot, your hunting area is sharply restricted, so you can't do much (or any) shooting until you get the primary animal.

hunt, especially if you're picky. The difference is that most of these animals are not hunted exclusively, any more than the common species are. The hunts that require serious concentration are hunts that require baiting or tracking and hunts for animals like sitatunga and mountain nyala, which occupy specialized habitat. I don't recommend any of them for a first-time hunter. Tracking hunts—with the exception of buffalo, because they are relatively plentiful—are exceptionally difficult. I don't mean physically (for me that's the fun part) but mentally. When you're tracking elephant, bongo, or giant eland for days on end, you are usually seeing very little other game, and in some cases no other game at all, day after day. It takes experience to make this kind of hunting more rewarding than it is exhausting and frustrating. Everyone is different, but I wasn't ready for that kind of hunting until I had a number of safaris under my belt.

When it comes to the great prizes—big elephant, bongo, giant eland, mountain nyala—you simply must put in the time, hunting these animals exclusively until you either win or run out of time. The day you decide you've had it and you try something different is the day you might have been successful. However, there's concentration of effort and there's also foolishness. When you're hunting the difficult animals you mustn't let yourself get sidetracked, but it isn't necessarily a good idea to pass up great opportunities.

Hunters have different philosophies on this. A true purist hunts only one animal at a time, and if anything else pops up he ignores it. A true opportunist follows the principle, "A bird in the hand beats two in the bush." In my thinking, neither course of action is exactly right. While hunting your primary quarry you can't get distracted by every animal that wanders across your path, or else you have no chance at the game you really want. But some opportunities are too good to pass. It's always a tough call, but you must weigh the odds and make the best decision you can.

Knowing that I have a history of getting sidetracked, when I made my first giant eland hunt I promised myself that I would shoot no other game until we got the eland. We didn't get the eland, and I got no other game. Period. Over the course of the safari I had opportunities at several unique Central African species that I had never hunted before, and it would have been nice to have some consolation prizes. Next time around things went perfectly: I got the eland halfway through the hunt, and in the remaining days took a good selection of the other game. But on that second hunt I can promise you I would have let myself get sidetracked if the circumstances had been right. For instance, I would have instantly broken off an eland track if we'd encountered a herd of roan—but I wouldn't have done that for waterbuck or western kob.

On my first bongo hunt I probably didn't stay as exclusive as I should have. Over the course of the hunt I took a wonderful giant forest hog, a buffalo, and a yellow-backed duiker. I didn't get a bongo, but I got pretty good consolation prizes and it was a great safari. On my second bongo hunt I think the only thing I would have broken off a track for is a forest sitatunga. I got the bongo with more than a week remaining, and although we continued to hunt hard, the one shot I fired at my bongo was the only shot I fired during the twenty-one-day safari!

I am clearly no purist, but I have never actually been faced with the decision to break off hot pursuit of a primary quarry in favor of a "target of opportunity." As a general rule it would be a bad idea to break off, but it depends altogether on what the opportunity means to you. I wouldn't consider

On any safari there will be slow days and days when game is everywhere. Just remember that hunting is hunting, and you're there to have fun. Each day you will see the sights you have long dreamed of, so enjoy it and take the good with the bad.

it for a common animal, even of huge proportions, but I wouldn't automatically dismiss a genuinely rare opportunity. In this situation, instead of the "bird in the bush" story, I think of the saying, "When Mother Nature smiles, don't kick sand in her face."

On every safari you should do as much as you can. To maintain a balance, try not to do so much that you hurt your chances for the game that is most important. It's a tough balance to strike, especially on the first couple of safaris, when every animal you encounter is a new experience. Keep in mind, however, that it is important to pay close attention to the animals that are only found in the area you are hunting.

Almost every African hunting area has at least a couple of indigenous species—animals only found in that region, or animals that are best hunted in that area because of availability, trophy quality, or both. At the outset you may not be particularly interested in these animals, but you might still be kicking yourself ten years down the road.

I've done a pretty good job in this department. From the outset I studied record books and other references, and I've always been pretty much aware of the game to be found in the areas I was going and in what other areas it could or couldn't be found. Almost without question, some of my priority animals, like lion and leopard, didn't get the attention they should have because I also wanted this and that. However, I've left relatively few things behind that I had to go back for. Most of these were animals that I just plain didn't get a chance at, part of those game lists that are never completed.

I have made a couple of colossal mistakes. In 1984 I hunted Zambia with Geoff and Russ Broom. We finished the hunt in Bangweulu, the only place black lechwe are found. I had just taken a huge Kafue lechwe. The black lechwe looks similar

It's easy to push yourself too hard on safari. Just being there is part of the fun, so relax and roll with the punches, and enjoy the campfires under the Southern Cross.

but has shorter horns. We saw plenty of black lechwe, but I was running short on trophy fee money and I wasn't mad about them. I didn't take one, knowing all the while that they only occur in Bangweulu. It was eleven years before I got back to Bangweulu to take a black lechwe. I have now been to Zambia's Kafue blocks three times, and I have not taken a Crawshay waterbuck—and that is the only place they can be hunted. I have seen some good ones, too. It isn't that the lack of this animal in my collection bothers me; I wouldn't go back to Kafue just for that—but it was foolish not to take one while I was there.

So I'll finish this discussion with two thoughts. First, while you should spend the bulk of your safari pursuing the animals that are most important to you, secondarily you should concentrate on animals best hunted where you are. There may come a time when you'll be glad you hunted them when you could. Second, while we all have budgets we must live within, once you're there, license fees and trophy fees are a bargain in comparison to a subsequent safari for game you could have taken and didn't! Our next chapter will deal with the ticklish subject of camp etiquette, manners, and politics.

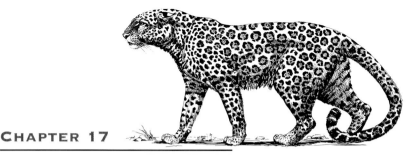

CHAPTER 17

SAFARI MANNERS

A happy camp is a successful camp. You can help maintain the magic!

African hunting differs little from all other hunting, and hunting differs little from most other endeavors. It isn't always within our ability to control the degree of success, but we can control how much enjoyment we get out of hunting, and attitude is everything. The most important thing to keep in mind is that you're there to have fun. Some days will be better than others. During the course of most safaris there will be delays, logistical problems, vehicle breakdowns, and just plain screw-ups. Your professional hunter may not always make the right decisions or orchestrate a stalk so that it works. The animals may not always cooperate. And you're going to screw up, too. My own mistakes tend to bother me more than most other things. I hate to miss—but when things go wrong it does absolutely no good to sulk. The best thing is to keep smiling, put problems behind you, and go forward. The next hour or the next day will be better if you allow it.

Professional hunters aren't altogether free of moods, either. Some are great conversationalists and some are hopeless introverts. A very few are there for the money, but most of them are there because they love the sport just as much as you do. Regardless of personality or motivation, African professional hunters are just that: professionals. They work incredibly long hours and stay out in the bush away from their families and homes for months at a time. Most of them earn very little money, and even the successful ones don't do particularly well in relation to the time and effort they expend. Whatever else they are, they are human, just like their clients. They can make mistakes, they can get angry, they can forget to take care of little details now and again. They also vary in experience and pure hunting talent. But I have never, ever met a properly licensed African professional hunter who didn't try to please his client to the very best of his ability.

That's really all you can ask. However, I think it's a two-way street. Your professional hunter has the right to expect you to do your best as well. On tough hunts you probably can't walk as far as he can, and none of us will make all the shots our PHs think we should have been able to make. But you can do the best you can—and try to keep yourself from bitching, complaining, and whining when things go wrong or get tough.

Your professional hunter is not your personal slave. He is in the entertainment business, and if he's good at his job he'll be aware of that. He will be a cordial host at mealtimes, and he'll sit around the campfire and tell stories, up to a point. But don't expect him to entertain you all night and hunt all day. Besides the care and feeding of his client, he is also responsible for the camp and staff and for the day-to-day hunting decisions that ultimately determine the success of the safari. He needs time to deal with the staff, keep the equipment running, think about how and where he should direct the morrow's hunt. And he needs rest. We're all different, so maybe he needs less sleep than you, maybe more. Don't expect or demand twenty-four hours of constant attention on each safari day. Take some books, magazines, or a battery-powered music system and some tapes, and plan on giving your PH some space.

We all hunt for different reasons and at different levels of intensity. It's your safari, so you can play it as you choose—but don't expect your PH to drink with you long into the night and then hunt all day. Your hunt will be far more successful,

You've hired your professional hunter for his experience and knowledge, so pay attention and let him use his skills.

Murphy's Law always applies. There will be problems and delays, and some will be worse than others. Don't get frantic. Chances are everything will "sort itself out" in due time. The hunt will continue, and will probably be successful.

as well as a whole lot safer, if he has his wits about him each and every hunting day. And if serious hunting is really your goal, you're better off to set a curfew for yourself as well.

Camp staffs vary significantly in both size and experience. Tanzania has the longest history of safari hunting. Camp staffs there tend to be very large, and some of the senior trackers, skinners, and camp managers may have decades of experience. When I hunted there in 1988 one of my trackers had tracked for my uncle clear back in '56. The level of experience is generally less in southern countries with newer safari

There are times when you can help out a bit, whether it's building blinds or loading game. You aren't expected to help, but you'll make points with both your PH and his staff if you do. Teamwork is important, and you need to become part of the team.

industries, and camp staffs tend to be smaller as well. This doesn't matter all that much; you will be taken better care of in any African hunting camp than anywhere else in the world. The trackers, skinners, camp managers, and cooks are professionals as well. They take pride in their work, and they, too, will work their tails off to make the safari as successful and enjoyable as possible. They are as deserving of your respect as the professional hunter. And if things go wrong and you must follow up a wounded animal, never forget that the trackers will go first—unarmed. Common courtesy and a friendly attitude go a long way—and these men rate it.

As the safari client, you aren't expected to do anything besides cover ground as well as you can and shoot as straight as you are able. Except under unusual circumstances, such as exceptionally long walks in extreme heat, I do recommend that the client carry his or her own rifle. This is simply because you never know when you might get a shot, and if an unexpected opportunity arises, it could be lost during the seconds it takes to transfer the gun. You are not required to pitch in and do actual work, any more than on any other guided hunt. However, I have found that helping with the skinning, butchering, and loading (or packing) of game—especially very large game that's difficult to handle—earns a lot of points with guides and guides' helpers the world over. Those points might earn a little extra effort when things get tough! Similarly, there may be occasions when it makes sense to pitch in and help. Obvious possibilities include setting up a fly camp with minimal staff or helping to free a stuck vehicle. You always have the option of sitting on your tail and being the bwana wa safari (master on safari), but anything you can do to make you, your PH, and the staff a team will help the overall effort, which, by the way, is intended to make your safari as successful as it can be.

Judging from the questions I receive, one of the great mysteries surrounding all guided hunting is this business of tipping. In

A successful professional hunter is a very good hunter, but he is also a good host and companion. Some PHs are more one than the other, and you can't change personalities in the course of a short safari. Go with the flow, and your PH will do the best job he knows how.

Africa, there are two sets of tips to worry about: first, to the camp staff; second, to the professional hunter(s). Tips to the camp staff should be considered absolutely mandatory. By our standards the costs aren't high, and the "gift" at safari's end is both a longstanding tradition and a fairly important part of the camp staff's wages. Most outfitters have a "range" of tips based on the length of the safari, and within that range there is usually some flexibility, based on both individual effort and results. For reasons altogether unknown to me, many professional hunters are likely to pass off tips with a shrug and a "whatever you think," but if you keep digging you can usually get them to come up with a figure that is average for that part of Africa.

Depending on how you feel about the safari, you can go a bit higher or a bit lower, but it is unwise to deviate too much from the professional hunter's recommendation. Too low is an insult; even if the results weren't what you hoped for, it would be very unusual if lack of effort on the part of the staff were to

Regardless of their duties, the camp staff will be well trained, and they will be proud of the job they do. Treat them with respect, and at the end of the safari remember them all with tips according to the local scale.

blame. Too high may raise the PH's expectations of the next client, who may not be as well-heeled as you are. There is also a definite hierarchy among all camp staffs, usually based on seniority, so most tips to camp staffs have a total figure and also a breakdown by individuals. If one staff member showed you extra effort or courtesy, you can reward that, but it's unwise to go overboard. You should clear with the PH any deviations from the standard tip schedule in a given camp, because he has to deal with any hurt feelings or staff politics after you leave.

Small presents like inexpensive watches, T-shirts, caps, and knives are greatly appreciated, but if you intend to go this route, find out up front how large the camp staff will be. Leaving somebody out is worse than bringing nothing—and do not expect that these presents will take the place of cash tips and save you a few bucks. That ain't the way it works! Store-bought cigarettes are a great luxury in Third World countries, so even if you don't smoke, pick up a couple of cartons at the duty-free shop. A pack or two a day to share among the staff is appreciated far more than you know.

Tipping your PH is a far less cut-and-dried matter. Nobody in the safari business is getting rich, and if your PH isn't the outfitter, he probably isn't making much more than a hundred bucks a day, regardless of what you paid for the safari. Heck, with outfitting costs as they are, even if he is the outfitter, he isn't making a fortune. So your tip will be greatly appreciated. Unfortunately, there is no standard formula like there is for camp staffs. Length of hunt and cost of hunt figure in, but the most important criteria are what you can afford and how you feel about the safari. In other words, there isn't much help out there, so most of us avoid getting specific about this issue. Colonel Bill Williamson of Fair Chase Ltd. is one of the few experts I have ever heard address this issue head-on. He has a great little booklet that he gives clients, and it suggests that an appropriate tip to a PH might be based on five percent of the daily rate. That's probably a good starting point. Williamson also points out that PHs have enough binoculars and so forth, and what they really appreciate is cash. I'm not altogether certain about that. Over the years I have given top-quality binoculars to several professional hunters. They still use them, and I believe the gift was appreciated and has lasted longer than the equivalent in cash would have. If you are considering something like that, take a look at the equipment the PH already has and make sure you're offering a genuine improvement and something he really needs, not just pawning off something you don't want. There are many kinds of tips, and they range from very modest to downright spectacular. What you do must be based on what you can afford as well as how you feel about the safari—but don't overlook this important bit of etiquette.

This is purely my opinion and my way of approaching things, which doesn't make it right for everyone. This also applies to the two remaining subjects I want to address, except that these last two may be even more controversial. The first is adherence to African game laws; the second concerns trophy expectations.

African game laws vary widely from country to country. It is altogether unreasonable to expect the visiting sportsman to be familiar with them. The professional hunter must be. Much of the testing required to obtain a professional hunter's license deals with knowledge of game laws. The licensed professional hunter is charged with adhering to them and ensuring that his clients do as well. This is part of the reason visiting hunters are required to engage a licensed guide in so many countries throughout the world.

I believe any professional hunter worthy of the name should uphold the game laws of the country in which he plies his trade. His clients should insist that he do so, and the PH should insist that his clients do the same. Again, the game laws vary tremendously from area to area. In some areas it is totally illegal

The many trackers with whom the author has hunted have been extremely competent and genuinely nice guys who are keenly interested in success. These are Pygmies from extreme southeastern C.A.R., great people with wonderful senses of humor.

to shoot from a vehicle; in other areas it is not. In some areas it is legal to hunt some species at night; in other areas it is not. Provided the license and/or trophy fees are paid, some areas allow more than one animal of some species; others allow only one to a customer. Some countries have minimum caliber restrictions; some do not. Hunting is not a perfect science and mistakes can be made, but I believe very strongly that professional hunters and safari clients should strive together to adhere to the local laws and maintain the highest standards.

I have heard so-called hunters brag about taking multiple animals on a single license, and there are videos on the market that are made exciting by purposefully wounding animals to incite a charge. The good news is that I believe such abuses are rare. Most professional hunters are extremely ethical and do their best to play by the rules. On the other hand, they are

There will be dead time on any safari, sometimes lots of it. Take some good books, a notebook, or whatever you need to do to occupy yourself, and take it easy. Hunting is rarely successful when you try too hard.

under tremendous pressure to please their clients. The best course is to discuss the rules of the road at the outset of the safari and then stick by them. While we safari clients—strangers in strange lands—may not know the local laws, most of us have more than enough hunting experience to know what is right and what is wrong. We must not discard the basic rules of ethics and sportsmanship simply because we're on someone else's turf, or because we have invested a lot of dollars in the safari. We as hunters have enough trouble, and it is imperative that we respect the laws of the African countries that still allow us to hunt.

While we are discussing the local laws on how you may or may not hunt, it's a good idea to bring up the subject of exactly what you may hunt and what you may not hunt. Chances are you booked your safari with certain animals in mind. There are almost certainly other animals in the area that you didn't think of at the time. Most areas today have fairly rigid game quotas, and some require up-front licenses, so you may be restricted to the animals you contracted to hunt. That should be just fine with everyone. But you don't know exactly what you might run into on a given day in Africa, so it's a good idea to discuss the "what ifs." Animals may be available that you hadn't thought about, and there may be unallocated quota. On the other hand, there may not be, but it's a good idea to ask the question; and you should also ask how much the trophy fee would be so that you'll know exactly where you stand. When an encounter occurs, it's usually much too late to discuss the possibilities.

On to the final issue. I think one of the more unfortunate aspects of modern hunting is the thirst for record-class animals. Mind you, this is not all bad, and it certainly doesn't have to lead to unethical behavior. Despite the fact that there is far less wildlife in Africa today than there was a half-century ago, average trophy quality continues to escalate. I don't think this is because animals are growing bigger horns, but rather because modern hunters are far more selective than they used to be. If you question this premise, gather up some old hunting books and look at photographs of

"Shoot him again!" Cartridges are cheap, but human lives aren't. American hunters are particularly bad about "admiring the shot" when they should be putting in an insurance shot.

safaris taken in the 1940s and 1950s. Yes, the elephant tusks were heavier, and the safari bags were much larger, but most of those antelope trophies are mediocre by today's standards. I'm sure that better trophies were available back then, but today's hunter and professional hunter are much more conscious of trophy quality. This is a good thing, and the world has Safari Club International and the excellent SCI record book to thank for it.

The problem is that I think we've gone a little too far. A superlative trophy is a wonderful thing—but "record-book fever" is not. All too often, at least for my taste, I hear the results of a safari described as something like "nine out of ten in the record book." An African safari is a grand experience, and surely there's more to the memory than how many times your name will go into the book!

Again, good trophies are wonderful, and I'm all for being as selective as the area and time will allow. If you want to set extremely high standards and seek only the very best trophies, I'm all for it, as long as you don't whine if you don't find what

It's OK to disagree, but hunting-camp politics are such that you'd better be certain you're right. The author thought he saw this Soemmerring gazelle drop to the shot. Colonel Negussie didn't see it and pointed out another similar male. The author refused to shoot, and the colonel was upset . . . until they walked up on the one the author had shot.

you're looking for. Or, worse in my book, you race for the downed animal with tape in hand, and if it comes up a bit short of what you expected, you don't like it anymore.

In the previous chapter I stated that it's unlikely that any hunter will fill the entire game list in a given area. It is also extremely unlikely that all of the animals you bag will be of record-book proportions. However, several probably will be. There are a number of reasons for this. First, the record-book minimum scores, whether SCI or the old Rowland Ward, are somewhat more lenient when compared to Boone and Crockett minimums for North American big game. Second, both safari clients and professional hunters are very much aware of trophy quality; the clients demand good trophies, and the PHs strive to find them. Third, while African wildlife suffers from poaching, predation, and habitat loss, there is actually very little hunting pressure as we know it. Especially in well-managed hunting areas, a good percentage of males live long enough to realize their trophy potential.

The average safari bag will include several record-class trophies. This is especially true on game ranches in southern Africa, where poaching and predation can be controlled and the harvest is a cash crop. However, they won't all make the book. This is because, regardless of the intensity of management, the different species thrive in different habitats. No one area is capable of producing top-quality specimens of all the game present. Also, few hunters possess that much luck! And, after all, if every single animal taken by every single hunter made the book, it wouldn't be much of a book, would it?

In my view there is nothing wrong with good, mature, representative specimens, regardless of their book measurement. So relax and enjoy your beautiful trophy. Remember the way it looked just before you pulled the trigger, the way you sweated during the stalk, and how hard it was to control the shakes when you brought up the rifle. These things matter much more than an inch of horn one way or the other. Later, if you wish, take out the tape and have a look. If your trophy earns you a place in the book, wonderful. If it doesn't, maybe you can look for a bigger one next time around—but in the meantime, who cares? It's still your trophy, and when it's on your wall it should still bring back fine memories of a beautiful day in Africa.

In our last chapter, we'll talk about trophy care and shipping.

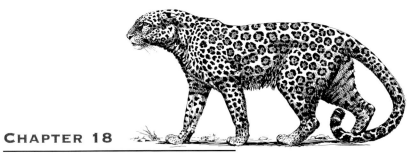

CHAPTER 18

GETTING THEM HOME

They're your trophies, so field care and shipment is your concern!

I hear the horror stories at just about every convention: tales about trophies that never arrived, came in with hair slippage, fell apart at the tannery, or weren't the same animals you shot. Funny, in this last instance I don't think anyone has ever told me that they received bigger trophies than they left in Africa! Nothing is ever absolutely certain about shipping trophies. One very competent taxidermist, a man I trust, told me once that something approaching a third of the trophies he receives from Africa come in seriously damaged. So I've been fortunate, which is not to say that I haven't had problems. In 1994 a shipment from Tanzania was seriously delayed when the outfitter's partner absconded with trophy fee payments rather than giving them to the government. I eventually received the trophies, but the skins had been exposed to humidity for too long, and most were ruined. This, unfortunately, is the kind of problem that is going to crop up now and again, and it's difficult to guard against.

Most of my difficulties have been much more bizarre and even more difficult to guard against. There was a good vaal rhebok that simply vanished off the face of the earth, sent but never received. Then there was a bontebok that, for whatever reason, wasn't shipped when it should have been. My CITES permit expired a couple of days before it arrived in the States. I called around and got a stay of execution, but it was too late. They burned my bontebok skin and horns before the contraband

The quality of skinning depends somewhat on the area and how experienced the staff is. Good knowledge of skinning is important for every hunter. Trophy care in Kenya was fabulous, and the entire staff was extremely experienced—but those days are largely over.

burners got the word. Finally, I had a wonderful nyala that arrived in the United States with just one horn!

This may sound like a lot of trouble for one person, but it isn't. I've made a tremendous number of hunts in Africa, and I've received many shipments of trophies, often comprised of just one or two animals. I'll talk a little more about the specific problems I've had, because some of them might have been prevented. First, however, we're going to talk about trophy care. Despite the losses just mentioned, I think I've been lucky. Other than that Tanzania shipment, I can't recall receiving a single skin from Africa that couldn't be mounted if I chose to. Sure, I've received a few skins that the taxidermist clucked over, but all could be repaired. The biggest problem with African trophies isn't excessive delays or losses in shipment but skins that were ruined long before they reached the expediter.

A typical skinning shed arrangement at Russ Broom's camp in Zambia. You don't want to make a pest of yourself, but the trophies are ultimately yours. It's wise to drop by the skinning shed every now and again!

This is not necessarily due to neglect on the part of your professional hunter and his staff, although it could be. When a bad skin comes back from the tanner, your taxidermist will probably phone you to give you the bad news. Needless to say, you will be angry, and you will want to fix blame. It is very unlikely to be your taxidermist's fault. All he did was receive dried skins and send them on to the tannery. It could be the tannery's fault; tanning is a rough process that involves some risk to skins, especially the thin hides of cats and smaller antelopes. The damage could well be caused by improper trophy care in camp or by exposure to weather while awaiting shipment. Chances are the outfitter and/or professional hunter will receive the blame, which may or may not be justified.

Even with the very best care, there is considerable risk, especially on rainy-season safaris or late-season hunts when the weather is extremely hot. And in any case, when the skin has massive hair slippage or falls apart during tanning, it is too late to worry about fixing blame. Taxidermists have a pretty good network, and it is usually possible to get a replacement cape if your skin turns out bad, but the more unusual the animal, the more difficult and expensive this is. The best course is to take all the precautions you can to ensure that your trophies reach you in good condition.

Since trophy care isn't a sure thing, there is nothing you can do to absolutely guarantee this. You can ensure that your trophies receive the kind of attention that should prevent spoilage. It's proper that you do so because, after all, your trophies belong to you. It is the professional hunter's duty to make sure your trophies receive the best care he and his staff know how to offer, but I believe much of the responsibility—and most of the risk—lies with the hunter. After all, it's you who will enjoy them for the rest of your life, and you might not, if they don't make it home in good enough shape to mount.

Too many safari clients leave trophy care altogether up to the professional hunter and camp staff. Under most circumstances, especially in Africa, it's appropriate that they do most of the work, not necessarily because trophy care is part of what you're paying for, but because they probably know how to handle your trophies far better than you do. But I firmly believe that every hunter who wants to have mounted trophies in his or her home should know how to skin, how to cape, and how to properly care for trophies under any conditions.

The occasion might arise anywhere, even in Africa—or perhaps especially in Africa—where you have to do it yourself. Because of the warm weather, the clock starts running when an animal is taken. If the skinner is sick or the PH has some urgent matter to tend to, you might need to pitch in and do the caping yourself. This would be extremely unusual. More important, if you don't know how to do it yourself, how can you be sure it's being done right? Mind you, as a paying client you do have a right to good trophy care. But things happen. You may wind up in the hands of a beginning PH, or for a variety of reasons there may not be a properly trained and experienced skinner in camp.

I do not recommend hovering over the skinner or making a nuisance of yourself. Casual and frequent trips to the skinning shed should tell you what you need to know. There is no magic involved; proper skinning is just a matter of slow, careful work. If you don't know how to do it, spend a little time with your taxidermist, and maybe practice on a deer or two close to home.

Skinning is just the first step. Heat and moisture, especially in combination, are the enemies. There is usually no way to refrigerate or freeze skins in Africa, so the only sound option

All of the spiral-horned antelope also have extremely fragile skins, complicated even more by the relatively short hair.

is salting and drying. The freshly skinned hide should be as clean as possible. Fleshing—removing as much as possible of the subcutaneous fat and any flesh remaining—is much more difficult and painstaking work than the initial skinning, but the cleaner the skin is, the less likely you are to have hair slippage. While the ultimate object is to completely dry the skin, water doesn't hurt a fresh skin. Blood will stain white or pale-colored skins, and you don't want dirt on the flesh side. So before the drying process is started, the skin should be thoroughly washed.

Salt is the key ingredient, and you need lots of it. Absent salt, it is possible to air-dry skins, especially in relatively cool temperatures with low humidity, but the risks are huge. Salt is the answer, because salt draws moisture. Any salt is better than no salt, but the finer the better because granulated salt can be worked into all the nooks and crannies, and it draws moisture better than coarse salt. Most skinning sheds will have a salt box, sort of like a sandbox filled with salt. Lay the wet skin hair down, and pour fresh salt onto the flesh side, then rub it in so that it gets into the edges, the lips, the nose, the turned ears. From a technical standpoint, bacteria breeds in moisture around the hair follicles, causing them to open and the hairs to fall out. That's hair slippage. Salt pulls the moisture out, allowing the hair follicles to seal. Every day or so the wet salt should be shaken off and replaced with fresh salt. Depending on the temperature and the thickness of the hide, in a few days the skin will be completely dry and as hard as concrete. Once it is completely dried—and kept dry—it will last just like that for several years. Skins that are properly dried actually have a longer "shelf life" than a tanned skin, and they can be tanned and mounted with perfect results at any time.

The primary issues are plenty of salt that is changed several times, and prompt care. Just how prompt depends on the weather and also on the animal. Cats are especially subject to hair slippage. They should be skinned and salted as rapidly as possible. Even with the best care, most lions won't have as good a mane after taxidermy as they did in life. The skins of all the spiral-horned antelope are also fragile and need prompt attention. This doesn't necessarily mean immediately, but an animal taken in the morning should be skinned and salted no later than midday. With African daytime temperatures, the evening is too late. In warmer weather, or if there is no plan to return to camp at midday, most professional hunters carry salt with them. Failing that, the skin can always be put in a cooler. So long as it is kept cool the salting can wait. When an animal is taken toward evening, even the skinning can wait until morning during the African winter. But when the weather is warm, especially when it is warm and humid, the clock is ticking rapidly.

In warm weather, trophy care back at camp isn't soon enough. Smart PHs carry a bag of salt with them, so animals can be skinned on the spot and salted before the hunt continues. This is a red-fronted gazelle on a hot day in southern Chad, so immediate skinning and salting was essential.

This means that you have to give your professional hunter time to care for the trophies. Depending on how robust the staff is, the morning after you take an animal you may stay in camp until the skin is properly salted. When you take an animal in the morning, you may take a lengthy break right there so the trophy can be skinned and salted and the meat cared for. This last is also important. While you may occasionally go out looking strictly for camp meat, you as a safari client are not meat hunting. But recovering the meat, whether for the camp, local people, or the local market, is an important part of the safari business. Sometimes it takes time, but that's OK. Wasting meat is just as unethical in Africa as it is anywhere else—maybe even more so, since most local populations are starved for protein.

Once you've taken your trophies and have ensured that they've had the best field care possible, the next step is to get them home and to a taxidermist. Or take the meat to an African taxidermist first. Let's discuss this decision.

Wherever you go, it's important to choose a competent taxidermist. You will look at your trophies for decades to come, and bad taxidermy doesn't get better with age. There was a time when African taxidermy was clearly inferior to American taxidermy. I had the trophies from my first safari mounted in Nairobi, and they weren't done very well. Today, however, there are a number of very competent African taxidermists, especially in the southern countries of Zimbabwe, South Africa, and Namibia, so quality isn't the issue. Taxidermy prices are generally quite a bit lower over there, reflecting lower labor costs and favorable currency exchange rates. The tradeoff is that the rates for air freight are based primarily on cubic measurement rather than on weight, so it is much more costly to ship mounted trophies than dried and folded skins, skulls, and horns. You can save some money overall, but not as much as you might think.

Moisture is the enemy because it breeds bacteria. Salt draws the moisture and allows the hair follicles to seal, so it is essential. Depending on the skin and the weather, salt needs to be changed several times until the skin is absolutely dry.

Cats are especially susceptible to hair slippage, and the skins are very fragile. Skinning and salting should be done promptly, and must be done with extreme care.

I have had some excellent taxidermy done in Africa in recent years, so I don't have a strong bias either way. However, there's one thing worth thinking about. At the conclusion of a successful safari most of us are in a foggy state of euphoria, especially after the first safari. We think our PH was the greatest hunter who ever lived, and we're delighted with all of our trophies. This is a very poor time to make decisions about which trophies to have mounted and which not to. Even today I know that I'm better off "cooling down" for a period, then figuring out exactly where I might have room to hang a trophy and making a sensible decision about what should be a head mount, what should be a European (skull) mount, and whether anything should really be done life-size. After all, not all of your trophies will be superlative in quality. Maybe you want the trophy mounted anyway to commemorate a great day afield. Or maybe you should hang onto the horns and skin and see if you get a better trophy of that species next time around.

The other consideration is that, if you select a taxidermist before your safari, he will be prepared to assist with receiving the shipment into the United States. He will provide tips not only on trophy preparation but also on what measurements he might want. Many taxidermists also provide trophy tags for your skins and horns. These are not essential, but they're a good idea and preclude inadvertent switching of trophies.

Mounted or not, your trophies will still have to be shipped home. The only sensible way to do this is air freight. Period. Don't even consider sea freight. It's cheaper but much slower. More important, the trophies are at much greater risk, not only from the elements, but because everything that delays shipment increases the chances of something going wrong. This is not to say air freight will be quick. Most outfits do their shipping after

At long last the crate comes from the taxidermist. Will you like the result? That depends on what happened in camp, and it's now much too late to do anything about it.

the hunting season is over, so the time lag between your safari and the arrival of your trophies varies from a few weeks to as much as six months.

Most outfitters use an expediter at the nearest international airport, and most do a pretty good job. It is, after all, a routine part of their business. All you can really do to help is make certain that shipping instructions are absolutely clear. Again, a taxidermist who deals a lot in international shipments can be invaluable. For Americans, trophy shipments must come to a port of entry for clearance. If you don't live near a port of entry, then a customs broker will have to clear the shipment for you. The cost is not high, and the money is well spent. The American safari market is large enough today that most African outfitters and freight expediters know exactly how to do all this, but it's always wise to ask the questions and make sure you understand exactly how your shipment will be forwarded.

Regrettably, you have very little control over the costs. There are few shipping options, so there isn't much shopping around to be done. Costs from southern Africa, where there are lots of flights and literally thousands of trophy shipments annually, are quite reasonable; shipping costs from more remote areas can be frightful. They vary quite a bit, but most shipments of unmounted trophies from southern Africa will run between $750 and $1,200 for several animals. On the other hand, the shipping for my bongo from Central African Republic—one animal, much shorter distance—cost $1,500. That was the worst shock I've ever had for shipping. Most of the time shipping costs have seemed quite reasonable, and they haven't gone up much in the past quarter-century.

The paperwork from the country of origin must be correct, including any required veterinary certification. Your outfitter will handle this, and you'll usually be charged a modest

At safari's end it's wise to review the trophies and make sure everything is properly tagged.

"dipping and packing" fee for the services. The only paperwork you are responsible for is any required CITES import permits. At this writing, CITES import permits are required for leopard, white rhino, bontebok, and elephant. Leave copies with your outfitter, but keep the original and make sure your taxidermist or customs broker has it when your shipment arrives. As I learned with my bontebok, the CITES permit has a shelf life. Keep in touch with your outfitter via phone or fax, and if your permit is approaching expiration, don't let him ship until you've gotten a new permit. Had I been paying attention, I would have known my bontebok permit was expiring. That one was my fault. The U.S. Fish and Wildlife import form must also be filled out, but a customs broker can handle that for you.

I have a feeling that small shipments of one or two trophies are at greater risk than a big boxful of stuff. Trying to send a tiny vaal rhebok cape and horns all by itself was asking for trouble, and I should have known better. If your shipment is small, consider trying to consolidate it with that of another American. Usually the shipping will be cheaper split in half, even if the number of trophies is doubled. Again, tags that clearly identify your trophies are good insurance.

Now, about that one-horned nyala. Someone who either doesn't like me or doesn't like my writing swiped the missing horn in South Africa. I don't know if I have ever met the person or not, but I know that's what happened because whoever it was, he has bragged about doing it and the word has gotten around. I don't know how you guard against something like that, but I believe that someday I will find out who among us was low enough to steal that horn! Meantime, despite the horror stories, I don't worry too much about whether my trophies will make it safely or not. I pay close attention to the trophy care, and I figure they'll turn up eventually. Over the course of a quarter-century, almost all of them have.

This is good because the trophies are important. They serve as tangible reminders of the wonderful experience that is African hunting. Every time I look at mine they bring back the kaleidoscope of sights, sounds, smells, and feelings that is Africa. And they help get me through the time until I can return to Africa once more.